I0119007

TRUTH

Written by

Roderick Howard

GLADSTONE PUBLISHING SERVICES
NEWARK, DELAWARE

Copyright ©2017 Roderick Howard

All rights reserved.

This book contains the personal opinion and beliefs of the author, and by no means represents the beliefs of the publisher or publishing staff. No part of this book may be reproduced or transmitted in any form or by any means, electronic or mechanical, including photocopying, recording, or by any information storage and retrieval system, without the written permission of the author.

Contact Information:
Roderick Howard rhoward@gladstonepublishingservices.com

Publishing Services Provided By:
One Smart Lady Productions Editing
Gladstone Publishing Services
Newark, DE 19713
info@gladstonepublishingservices.com

Second Edition

10 9 8 7 6 5 4 3

ISBN-13: 978-1928681-37-3 (paperback)

ISBN-10: 1-928681-37-9

Printed in the United States of America.

Dedication

I want to dedicate this book to Trayvon Martin who was killed by the neighborhood watch volunteer. May he rest in peace.

Dedication

Contents

§§§

Preface

"Truth" written by Roderick Howard follows the philosophy of relativism (relative truth), a doctrine where there are no absolute truths. With relative truths, things can be described, understood and accepted based on culture, ethnicity, language, and social upbringing. The truth is relative to the frame of reference or point of view of the communicator. Today we see many of the younger generations; Generation X, the Millennial, and those coming into the Age of Reasoning (teenagers) seeking separate paths from their elders to understanding their past and their purpose. In this post-modern time, this community has adopted truth relativism which allows them to follow a plurality of truths based on their understanding.

"Truth" is written by a self-educated scholar. It is based on Roderick Howard's extensive research and his quest to understand the world in which he lives. He continues to seek and understand how and why the information, according to the post-modern philosophers, taught in our public and catholic schools are so flawed. He continues to seek a way to bring those in society, who do not desire to follow the Absolute truth taught by their Elders, into active participation and prosperity in today's society, and have them no longer treated as outcasts.

The truths revealed in this book will facilitate many discussions for those who were raised to believe in Absolute truths, such as the Bible being the inspired Word of God, those who stand by our government right or wrong, and those who seek the true ancestral histories of a people of colour stigmatized by slavery, apartheid, and modern day racism. For those who hold to the traditional ways of worship and traditional institutionalized philosophies, in some sections, Roderick Howard's "Truth" will be a difficult read. I invite you to read it to gain an understanding of the truth relativism which our younger generation today builds their foundational beliefs. Somewhere during the conversations, this book will trigger, I pray that hearts and minds will open up to discuss ways to eliminate hatred, violence, and misunderstanding between generations and culturally different groups.

For me, I believe in the Absolute truth of the inspired Word of God. In 2 Timothy 3:16-17 it tells us, "All Scripture is inspired by God and profitable for teaching, for reproof, for correction, for training in righteousness; so that the man of God may be adequate, equipped for every good work." This is the truth I follow in my private and professional life.

I also believe we must give a voice to those who are typically shut out of society, even those who are labeled mentally ill, unstable or misfits. Many violent individuals have reached out for help, yet were turned away because they could not vocalize their thoughts. Roderick Howard writes about these people and this truth in his book. The Bible says in Proverbs 4:7 "Wisdom is the principal thing; therefore get wisdom: and with all thy getting get understanding." We must work hard to understand those who are different from us religiously, culturally, ethnically, emotionally, and mentally.

Deborah Smart
Publisher and Author

Introduction

"I was born in the city of Camden, New Jersey. I attended Northeast Elementary School from Kindergarten until the 5th Grade. I then attended a Junior High School called Pyne Point; located in Camden from 6th to 8th grade. I attended 9th to 12th grades at Camden County Vocational School in Sickler-ville, New Jersey until I graduated.

It is important that my book reaches people of this modern society that are going through situations that come with life's obstacles by giving them principles and elements that can be applied to their foundation."

Roderick Howard, Author

Truth

Chapter 1
Truth As I See It.

Truth has to continuously be told just as the rain, snow, sleet or hail never stops. We all may recall when the days and nights were long and harsh. We all can recite months and weeks where we had to push harder and work extra hours to pay a bill or a child's college tuition. We all long for days when we can be care and worry free, but they never come. Lights get cut off where they normally shine. Our days are now crowded with the five devils that cheer with victory.

We become angry and madness starts to settle in. We look for a place to shield us from misery but don't find it. We adapt but don't like nor do we enjoy the person we have become. We become a part of people, places, and things that are negative, but in the eyes of the beholder, it looks and feels right.

We begin to lose our cause. We began to lose our purpose. Our vision is replaced and our hearts begin to harden. We start to put the blame on others. We look for the wrong answer that sounds right to the deaf and a visual sighting to the blind. No one can understand. No one can relate. No one can feel the pain nor the hunger we are going through. Or is it just oneself closed up and scared to go into the shining light ahead of them?

Everybody's path is different and their shoes are different sizes. Not all sheets are silky and not all beds are warm. We sometimes look for weapons that destroy a future and technology that invades. We sometimes work out to see if we burn off the anger. We sometimes sleep longer just to see if the days pass faster.

Are we scared of the truth? Are we in denial and have become comfortable with the person we have become? Are we scared of happiness or not ready for the challenge? Some visit psychologists and begin counseling because we try to cope with their childhood. Marriages begin to become a disaster and love does not live in the heart anymore. Where do we hide and where do we go? Where can we find a place to exhale and will not be judged because of past history and past events? Where can we go while in the mind of the negative formation? We do not regret what we have done but we learn from our experiences; it was either right or wrong.

An older crowd may look at the younger crowd like they are doing something wrong and do not know what they are missing. Is it that they, the older crowd, cannot relate to the times, and are in the stages of denial, not wanting to accept the fact that they, the older crowd, are older and their time is passing? Or, should they accept that it is their time to teach? The younger crowd is looking at the older crowd like they can't do it like us, or move as fast as us, or be hip like us. Or, should they recognize the experience of the older crowd comes with wisdom and understanding of life's up and down.

What kind of teachings can be taught if the minds of individuals are being misled, seductive to misunderstandings, violence, and misery? What kind of teachings or philosophies can be taught for a deaf person to hear? What kind of paintings or images may be created so the blind can see? And what words are motivating and inspirational so a dumb person starts making sense?

It was once said, "We go in fast forward…never rewind." But, time does repeat itself. War does not stop and victory is always rewarding; so why don't we want freedom? Fights only erupt in one's own misunderstanding of another's war. It only began because of someone else's greed for power.

Why not peace? Why not justice? Why not freedom? The thing that we do or say our future sees and hears. When they start to imitate our very same actions, we get upset, and can only blame our own irrational thinking. We can only blame ourselves for not showing our future what Dr. Martin Luther King Jr., Gandhi, Confucius, Mandela, and many other leaders have taught about peace. We can only blame ourselves for not finding a way out of the stages of confusion and express the meaning of life in a different fashion.

Can we accept change? Can we accept the fact that all people are not equally treated fairly? Are we against freedom and oppression and destruction? Can we acknowledge brotherly love is the only cure to happiness?

Do we accept failure or breakdown because of unexpected events? But have you thought of happiness being one of the roots to evil? We still look for happiness. It can flow through a thought in our mind that is filled with a passion of love. We crave it. Even in the midst of war, we crave for it. It is not only for the opposite sex, it is of the same sex. It comes unconditionally, and it is built with memories that are priceless.

We feel alone without it. We may feel separated from the outside world and crave for the internal emotion that manifests love. Somehow someway negative thoughts come about. Energy becomes stronger in a fashion of pain. Silence becomes the song. Darkness and loneliness settle. Future becomes shorter and days become longer. Those who have a spiritual energy have a vibe that is so positive it can be seen physically, as well as, emotionally.

Chapter 2
The Laughter. The Love.

The peace and the freedom can be felt through the words of the voice and the step with each foot. When the wind blows the hair stands to the breath of fresh air and smiles begin to shine upon the faces of the bright. The energy can be transferred into the negative and the unhappy person. It has an ability to push the gloomy clouds of a rainy day, and produce a rainbow while the sun shines upon the faces of the lonely, and the flowers and the plants upon the earth that God himself has created. Feeling good about oneself is a feeling that the weak does not like. It's like the devil is jealous and wants to bring the indigenous to a kingdom of love, peace, and happiness. But the passion of God and knowing thyself is an endless feeling that is always seen. It can be hereditary. No one is born emotionally impaired, so we all feel some sort of pain, happiness, sorrow, laughter, and madness.

Truth be told men deal with pride while women are too proud. Our men's pride is guarded with ego, and women are guarded with standards. Some men think they know it all while some don't know enough. Some women have been through a lot of which they never speak about, and some women haven't been or seen anything.

We all want to take the world by storm and feel as though no umbrella is required. But we tend to forget that all storms are not the same. Some days you get unexpected obstacles that slow you down or even make you lose sight of your vision or goal. While other days are long and hard, where by the end of the day you haven't accomplished your destiny for that day. We still strive for another day, while we are just blessed by God to wake up and start it with a planned addendum. So we give thanks and move forward.

I spoke to a fella and he began to tell me what he writes in his journal. He began to say how he starts speaking about the Illuminati. I asked, did he know anything about Master Masons and what they represent? He said, he did not.

If you do not know the beginning of any story, how could you know what the end is? We always must start from the starting point, then go at a pace that is equal to how we move and handle life. Moving too fast can complicate things. As we go throughout life we tend to beat ourselves because things don't go our way. Things don't always go as planned. Some things don't add up right. The harder you work the better things come out, right? Know and understand life is difficult depending on how you live it. Nothing really goes as planned. Some things always come up from your past or are just obstacles in the path that you are taking.

We must know putting all our apples in one basket cannot work. We must not overwork ourselves and become restless. Mistakes come about and stress to the body does not help. We must remember no one is perfect. Appreciate the things that we are blessed with and thank your creator for allowing you to see things clearly.

Never take advantage of anything, and never rub in the faces of people who don't have the things that you have. As easy as you gain them, they can be taken. The truth is you must treat them how you want to be treated.

They say in order to get respect you must give respect. Some give it but don't even give it back. Even though we may get upset and things that other people say may hurt us, we sometimes have to let it fly, especially if it does not apply.

God has a way of dealing with those who are ignorant to the facts of life and take things for granted.

Chapter 3
We Speak About Life.

As I said before, life is unpredictable and the road we choose has to be the road we stay on. Now some people pick the wrong road for personal reasons and others pick the right road according to their situations or status of life. Changes in life, such as dealing with the death of a member of your family or friend. We do live knowing death is to come, but we must live life to the fullest and have fun and enjoy the fact that we are alive regardless of condition we are in.

Criticism can be kept to oneself. A person that is not content with their self is the one who is lost. They want to find themselves but don't know how. They are use to the stages of being repetitive about living. If broken or done in any different fashion, reality sets in and negative thoughts began to occupy the mind of the lost, but not the weak.

We all are lost before we find ourselves. Some need the opposite sex for that extra push. They say you need to love thyself in order to love or attempt to know someone else or a significant other. At the same time, people may know where to look, and the road to take to get there, but the past may be not allowing you to proceed with your travels. It's crazy how the power of a woman can complete a man in all shapes, forms, and fashions.

It's crazy how we look for love in the opposite sex knowing and understanding either the thing can happen with that mysterious emotion called love.

You can feel that positive emotional energy that is felt from your significant other. It's like a parent's unconditional love, or it has an evil side to it; an oppressive attraction that is only separated by death. Now can you say love is the root of all evil? Everybody wants it and will do anything to for it. Some people will go to the end of the world to possess that emotion from another. Some become suicidal because they don't have it. Some develop health issues because they don't have it, miss it or just have the need to want it but can't find it.

That feeling is the deepest manifestation of emotions possible. It can make a person feel complete with it and lonely without it. So the question is, why do we search for the thing that makes us complete, and has an evil side to it, and we'll do just about anything to have it?

We must remember money can't buy you love. It can make things a little easier but you are lonely with or without love.

Now we think about ourselves as individuals being in situations where we are isolated from day one. If they are by our side devoted and loyal, and even though thoughts of faithfulness begin to travel through our mind, we begin to think negatively.

We say all we have is our dignity and pride. Not too proud to admit depression, but too strong to fold. We say at the end of the day, we are who we are and can't be broken. What doesn't make us, breaks us? We are not the ones who lose, they are.

Truth By Roderick Howard

It's a learning lesson in life with relationships when seeing our soul mates who are just by our sides because of who we represent, or how we treat people.

Chapter 4
We Speak About War
Without and Within.

When we think of war, we think of many things that seem justified and right. To have the heart to kill we must be in the right frame of mind and be strong about it. They say it's culture.

What about the lives that are being destroyed? What about the lifestyles, tradition, and culture that is carried from generation to generation? What about the children who sees destruction and start to develop a hatred for those who they feel do not respect the land or way of life? What about their religion?

We force democracy on others. We force knowledge that is not right or heard on others. We destroy and rebuild a nation that may be improper to their civilians. People who were once there and we expect them to lose what they once knew and practice and have them adapt to what we feel is best for them, as though it is peaceful and pleasant.

Confucius taught peace is the way through madness and confusion. Fighting only leads to war and destruction, and peace is lost forever. During World War II, the bombing of Pearl Harbor was devastating. Nearly 2,500 American soldiers died and 1,000 civilians passed helping the war. When it was all over, the Japanese were feeling a little regretful and stated, "a brilliant man is a man who can stop the war without fighting."

Even in the midst of war and destruction people still have heart and think about the lives that are being lost more than those who are winning. People lose loved ones and never really recover from the hurt and the pain inflicted by the ones who do not know them or their way of life.

Some are bred for war. Some are bred to be patriotic. Some are bred to be survivors. But, can you heal the hearts and minds of those who mourn because of someone else's stupidity? It is only when we get put into situations like incarceration that a person thinks about their own actions and the destruction that was done.

Now let's say this incarceration does not rehabilitate everyone. Sometimes it only makes matters worse. It has been said, once as we lose control of ourselves, it takes less stress to produce more reaction. Eventually, a complete loss of self-control leads to shock or sickness which kills us.

We must learn to reverse this state of affairs so that it will take more stress to produce less reaction. If we continue to go along the old way, we lose our ability to face the smaller issues of life. But, if we learn the new way of meeting life, we grow and adapt as greater challenges arise. We have been given the inner strength, the judgment, the power to overcome life's down points. But, if we do not know ourselves and we do not touch the inner strength, our judgment becomes blurry and we may approach things with caution instead of confidence. Confusion can cause chaos and an unpleasant outcome. Without being able to come to an understanding, the plague of rage may spread amongst the people and disaster may appear heavier than normal. The knowledge of one's self will help you understand who you really are. You can't read a book and discover yourself, but you can find a way to start.

The morals and respect that you are raised with show you how to respond to things in life. You approach things with a way of manners and respect, having the desire to achieve more.

Some have not been taught these principles. They do not know how to act with the respect to elders. Some, who are not raised that way, may still manage to gain the aspect of life and to deal with situations that come from misunderstandings and take into account other people's feelings and visions on issues. People may not like being wrong, let alone being told what to do.

Chapter 5
Ego Issues.

Too many chiefs and not enough Indians. Everybody is not born a leader, but leadership is needed and is very important. As I said before, it's lonely at the top and a shame to be at the bottom. No matter what position you are in or play, you have to try not to fool out. Every vote counts.

A person once said, "Why does the all mighty allowed humans to have devilish desires of envy, greed, and aggression?" One person said it was all because of the forbidden fruit from the tree of life. But didn't God say, "man is like one of us to see good and evil." We have now the ability to judge. Even though we do see good and evil as well as teach it, our judgment is sometimes in the way. We sometimes go off our gut feelings. We don't think things all the way through. Either it is an influence of the opposite sex or the fact we just want to fit in or get noticed.

Once the war is over, we then sit back and say to ourselves, "I should have done it a different way or sung a different tune." That's when we reflect on ourselves. Look in the very same mirror of truth. We search for things that are within ourselves.

We all want attention. We all want to shine. With the most of us, these desires are fleeting and easily quieted. We lose ourselves coming through life. What we are facing we have become. Our focus is so off we sometimes forget what our goals were as a young adult.

So we look for things in others. It has been said, our desires for another person almost always involve social consideration. We attract those who are attracted to other people. They sometimes fill in the gap or hole that appears in the heart and more or less in the mind. People are more complicated than the faces they put on in front of others in society.

A person who seems noble and persuasive could be disguising a dark side which will come out in a manner which is strange. If his or her persuasive ways are lies, manipulative, and dealing with deception it will, in fact, come out in the long run. What doesn't come out in the wash comes out in the dry. So people use what they are familiar with.

Chapter 6
Charisma.

It has been said, the essence of charisma is an overpowering emotion that communicates itself in a person's gestures, the tone of voice, in ways that are the most powerful for the unspoken. Express what others are afraid to express, and they will see the greater power in you.

Reach for the stars. Love life and express the happiness and joy you feel. No matter what situation that you are in, know that there are greater days ahead. Rainy days are just a challenge to our everyday struggle. We carry memories of our fallen leaders, gurus, soldiers, and warriors. They all fought for the same causes. The pursuit of happiness.

They say love thy enemy and the victory is won. So easily said than done. It is always a battle against the unjust. A battle for the reason and logic. A purpose. It's for the power but still fill low inside. That misery and its company. We deal with it in our own way of life.

Religion, protest, world domination, and new world order. Things are in front of our faces and under our noses but our minds are trained to see otherwise. We are programmed to fall in line and anything other than the program is unbalanced. We look for material things that can replace certain memories that can't be buried. Certain protocols to fall in line, and anything other than the program is unbalanced.

Unrighteous deals, with provisions and restriction laws, come into play. They are written by those who don't follow them themselves, and somehow are justified by dishonesty and disloyalty. They only think of themselves and get upset when justice is not served or they do not get their way.

Chapter 7
What Motivates Us?

We look for material things that can replace certain memories that can't be buried. Certain protocols and rules start to be filed. Questions now come about and only specific answers are given and some are avoided. Money is given out for hush-hush because consequences are given for situations that can are not be closed. Is the devil a liar or is it the truth being told by him and getting blamed for past actions? Do we forget about it or do we overlook it because of fear from within? The fear of freedom. The fear of being misguided or misled.

Motivation. The Freedom of speech. The right to protest. The right to express who you feel can never rest. Even Abraham Lincoln expressed how he felt about things that were going on then and made the 14th and the 15th amendment. Even though people disagreed with John F. Kennedy on how he felt, the American people were having mixed feelings about Dr. Martin Luther King Jr., and what his movement was about. The movement expressed that freedom must be given.

We overcome interracial relationships. We overcome racism from the north to the south. Racism still lives in the heart of several groups of people. We overcome slavery and we overcome injustice in the court system. Some courts and rules are still against certain groups of people. We as people have realized what is tearing us apart as a country and decided to deal with unity more than before.

Now as I say these things, all states and the counties still deal with the minds that are programmed because of their ancestors have betrayed them. Strong and unite only amongst selves who believe in the same thoughts and feelings that they feel. They all deal with capitalism, communism, patriotism, liberals, democracy, republicans, democrats, and world takeover.

Are these groups the ones that are separating themselves because they have a different way of looking at something? Or because they want to be on top, to be noticed as some kind of leader across the globe? Some have a way of expressing their ways of looking at people who do not follow the same teachings.

As they mount war and force their religion and way of life upon the weak. Some build and destroy, and some mount peace, love, and happiness to one day to take the world by storm and realize this is the only way to go. Some deal with frustration where they think the only way to let it be known how they feel is to start disruption amongst people and cause chaos.

We say karma has its way of coming back, sometimes faster than we may notice. So we must cherish what we are blessed with and not take advantage of what is given to us knowing it can be taken from us in a heartbeat.

Bad karma has you involved with someone who is stressful about things in their life and don't want to ask for help from anyone. Even when you attempt to give advice or give help because the stress or depression can be seen on their faces and bodies movement; they deny it. They say it's not it or it's nothing, but as they were raised they were taught to always be strong and express no weakness, but what one doesn't realize is denying help can cause a situation to get worst or deepen the depression and even cause them to become suicidal. They start pointing the finger at those who deal with strength and do not need much help.

These people take out their frustration on others and call it right. Their thoughts become unnoticed and their horrific actions start to come into play. We as people have to always give help if we can. Never turn your back and say to yourself, "They will be okay." If you spot a problem lend a helping hand.

Chapter 8
The Circle Of Life.

It may take a lifetime to figure out, but we love it. Regardless, what obstacles come with it. No matter how down we get and no matter how far up the ladder we are, we still appreciate the gift of life we are blessed with.

When we wake up in any part of the day from a long or restless hour, we may wake up sort of moody. We then look around and may not like our position. We may have overslept. We then wait for one person, regardless of who they are, we take out how we feel about them. Cursed words, negative statements, and anger come from the mouth of the one who is just frustrated with the situation they are waking up to.

Some apologize later and others deal with that pride thing and feel as though they are not wrong, and don't have to say anything. But it is the other person's actions who are wrong, even though they may be right. They have to feel good somewhere inside of themselves, and the only way to do so is to put down another person's feeling and attempt to belittle that person.

The devil also works in mysterious ways. They don't ask for help. They are stubborn. They then become filled with anger and jealousy. They compare their situation with yours and some become misfits. They look for a way out but cannot find one themselves. They deal with their problems by using and abusing others. They respond, not feeling loved, but they use or abuse others.

They do not feel loved or they are upset because what they planned to do did not come out how it was supposed to, and so they shatter the dream and love of another.

The sounds of birds. The smell of green grass. Just an attitude. I've been a grouch; even Mr. Grinch. You ask, "How do I change my heart?" Never live your life making others miserable. Find a hobby that keeps your mind elevated, where you are calm. Stay elevated. Keep the mind sharp by reading. Play board games that challenge you.

We must keep up with the times and always be aware of new technology. Meditation is good. Exercise your mind. We must find ourselves before we can attempt to understand the thinking of someone else.

As was once said, without any motivation and not to express his best the matter in the maze of exercises and the laws of deception. We cannot see the truth so we find it difficult to make a wash let alone and this isn't for ourselves.

We as humans do not sweet talk before thinking, and we do speak and usually it's something about ourselves. We use words to express our own feelings, ideas, and options. Reason being; we are generally self-absorbed, the person who is just as much as our inner self. We all share emotions and no one feels inferior to someone who speaks, who serves up their feelings. You must make your voice an instrument and train it to communicate emotions.

Allow yourself to be heard respectfully. Every time we are annoyed or whatever the reason is, we always feel as though we must follow through with a chain reaction of emotionless thoughts, words, and deeds, everyday life becomes more negative. Understand positive thinking comes as a gift from God; the power to know good, and evil. Genesis 3:22.

The motives have a lot to do with all actions of men and women, even children. If you as an individual have not found your inner self, that is the center of the point of self-control. You cannot be objective to what you feel, what you do, what or who you are becoming. A man or woman will sell control of knowledge of self and understanding things without reason, control, fear, or die.

It is only the absence of what one is seeking will they go into a pattern of anxiety. External knowledge is not the answer. That is why it cannot be found in places where you're looking. It all lies within understanding and self-control, as well as, the knowledge of oneself. This is only brought into view by the love of Truth and the desire to move on according to spiritual principles.

Some people deal with life with anger. They are hurt and deal with feelings so much they become angry and upset with themselves and in their sickness to control things they cannot. Some people struggle to maintain security and a sense of relief in their lives.

The world is full of temptations. We must see people who have more than we do. The adventure and laughter they have in their lives. They have discovered riches and happiness. But we have weaknesses vulnerabilities and mental struggles. Whatever it is, it is something we cannot control. It is something that affects our everyday life. And I suppose we have a hard time getting around.

We then take it out on those who we love. We may have our jobs later from the damage that has been made from an illness and some frustration. That's why I just said, we learn from our past in order to feel what it is going on at the present time and can help see the future without making the same mistake as in the past. We look to the future. We look for a reason, a reason to live, a reason to love, and a reason to pursue our happiness dreams and goals.

The generations that I carried on my ass are loved ones to change, making the world a better place. But not everybody is on the same path. Some choose injustice and justice because none of those will listen to the reason that haunts them as guilt, or chips on their shoulders whenever we are told how to live rightly at any given moment. They change all situations and blame others for the end result and say it wasn't supposed to happen like that.

We don't look or own actions and elevate ourselves. We change our environment and move to a different area and think that will change. We figure being involved with a different relationship with help. The mirror never lies.

Now for some who feel as though they are the problem and their own enemy, they change places and maybe it's good. Old relationships may be the issue. But you may not be in denial and you cannot recognize the issues going on around you. No substance influencing the body can make you avoid reality. Sometimes it's a power struggle a legal issue that clouds the mind and control always come into play.

No one wants to feel like they don't have control. They have to be in the position where they call the shots and are always right. Some carry grudges and take it out on another or innocent. Some don't feel like they get the recognition that they are supposed to.

So now they feel like they have something to prove. The truth is only half the battle. Doing something with it is what most are after. No one likes the truth but the fact is what's right is right and what's wrong is wrong. Sometimes the truth can't hurt us but knowing what the truth is crossing the finish line of a journey and started a new battle.

As we know the truth, we think about life; our purpose and God's creation. Understanding the circle of life and the 360 Rotation is complete. You figure out some animals are born to be eaten by other animals. Just to survive. Bees pollinate and other plants grow. Cheese blows with the wind to shred seeds, unlock the floors, and grass is not only to look good, it is fruit for the animals such as antelopes. The circle of life we say. Everything has its purpose and cause of living.

We have to figure it figured out. Yes, it is this, and all that is said and done is a quest that comes with truth. Not alone, the journey is a spontaneous one. We join fraternities, cults, churches or groups of commissions looking for the one thing we call truth.

Peace is truth. Freedom is truth. Equality is truth and love is a secret truth. All comes with the circle of life. We do things to fit in with others. Styles. Ways of talking. Actions and reactions. We still move in a way that makes us feel comfortable. We do things to get that approval of others and the benefit of a doubt not to be talked about in a negative fashion.

Chapter 9
All Are Different For A Reason.

Everyone plays their own individual part of life. Your actions affect everyone. Some in a positive way and some in a negative way, but the whole objective is to be you. If someone else in the circle is not complete, things become complicated. You begin to lash out.

Stress also arrives and strength becomes your weakness. Honor and courage begin to fade into the dark. Guilt and negative thoughts flow through the mind and the heart becomes cold. Redemption, confessions and finding your true self is the key to having a prosperous beginning. Honesty to yourself is not allowing any worse that come from the outside affect your circle.

Beauty starts within. Never let the clouds of darkness cover your shine. We can never allow our own vision to be blurry to where we can't see the rainbow.

As I said obstacles come with life. Is it the inner strength and the fact of knowing yourself ? How you overcome minor mishaps and see what's over the mountain. We cannot continually clean ourselves because of our childhood. We cannot continue to blame ourselves when things go wrong. When a left turn leads to a dead end, turn around and make a right turn. You have to understand the road never ends but only begins again. Experience. Life cycle. Rape. Pain and pleasure. Mountains, Hills, Treetops and others who pass over. All are a part of life as we know it. Tears of joy, laughter and chaos. All our emotions and sometimes can't be explained. Sometimes can't be controlled. Sometimes it can be expressed and away and be hurtful or helpful.

They say the tongue is a double-edged sword because it can hurt as well as heal. It can be passionate or pleasurable. I can be deep as well as strong.

Followed by the mind and heart. Some say to follow your heart but the heart sometimes leads you to a dead end. They say listen to your gut feelings but that feeling could be spotted by fear. Voices could be silent because we don't have the courage to voice our opinions. Courage cannot be hidden because of the dark or we feel weak and can't go on anymore. Every space must be filled with hope. Lessons of experience that was self-employed only to be told the others who want to learn and listen. People have said put the truth in books because others will not pick them up to read it.

We have to take knowledge born in the mind of others and in our mind, as well as, in the mind of our children. Yes,we have to change ourselves in order to make a difference, but it's the future, our children, that keeps that difference going. No more lost legacies. No more hidden truth. No more leaders speaking only of inspiration.

This time we live in a time of the Apocalypse. Why? Not only have things developed to slow us down and kill us off we have been brainwashed by old and new technology, false teachings, fewer school days, more welfare

We commit disasters amongst ourselves because of pride, greed, lust, envy, gluttony, wrath, sloth, and the lack of knowledge. We say what is not right. We say what is not fair. People deal with manipulation, deception, smoke screens, and modern day slavery. But we are full of bills, work, and modern day activities. We may not have time to research or keep up with what's going on around us more or less in us. We are all humans and yes we are entitled to mistakes even the fact that we lose ourselves on the path of our choosing or based on the hand we are dealt or overcoming a habit that is picked up along the way and is even hard to break. But we try, try to forget about the past, try to forget about the mishaps, and try to forget about the slander that destroys us mentally because of hatred, jealousy, and envy.

Some of us are workaholics and choose not to deal with reality or not want to face the music thinking money will change things. Not knowing we are losing time away from families and quality time becomes a problem. Marriages begin to fail because we lose sight of what we were once set on in the beginning stages of our journey.

The death of one's friends or family member is a pain explainable but expressed deeply. It ranges from tears of pain to tears of joy. Knowing that the person or thing is no longer going through, but the memory that passes now lives within one's self. We relive words that were once said, and jokes that were once said, and jokes that were once heard.

Laughter still must go on because in the physical they are no longer here but in the spiritual. They stay with us. They are the little voice that tells us to do right things, make the correct choices, or gives us the courage to go hard when we feel weak and congratulate us on a "job well done".

We then move in a manner that would be approved by the ones that have passed. We may not have anything to prove but just want to make that person proud. Even in the light, some look at death as pain, while others look at it as glory. They beat life by accomplishing the things they wanted to do and the things they never dreamed of doing and passed happily instead of miserably.

   As I said before, life is short. We all want to live forever knowing we live to enjoy it and die when our time is up; expectedly or unexpectedly.

Chapter 10
United We Stand, Divided We Fall

Instead of uniting and working together to create solutions to cancer, disease, autism and many other human threats to the body, as well as, global warming, world overpopulation, deforestation, and many more. We worry about trilateral commitments, Consul of Foreign Relations, Bilderberg Groups, Jason Societies, and all of groups and societies that control things that we don't see, and yet we hear about religious wars and disputes on what was here first not knowing there are other ways of life many years before our current religions.

Media only mentions a little instead of the entire truth because (1) they don't want the whole truth to be known, and (2) people of society cannot handle nor accept the truth. Why? Because the people now pinpoint who are actually causing the corruption being disputed. Everything that is and was created to control the people by putting them into groups, by brainwashing the people, would collapse and chaos would erupt.

How do they control the people or groups of people who react in ways of violent behavior, or just try to push back the actual oppressor? It's called the police force. Law and constitutions that we live by are not only to keep things on track where we can be controlled but to make sure the economic portion of this is always funded.

The 13 Amendment was not even for a certain group of people in which slavery was not abolished until Abraham Lincoln felt like he was losing the civil war. Even after that, it was not really over. The Bill of Rights was written by 13 important people at the time and included Freemasons which all knew about who the law actually applied to.

It was the Dred Scott case which started to open the eyes of the people and the question about equality came into play. By this time the law, Bill of Rights, Amendments, and other government slavery was always mapped out up and running. Now we say we are all equal. Justice is blind and always will be.

Whatever happened to the treaty between the Moorish Americans and the European Americans? Why was the Statue of Liberty given as a gift from the French?" Why were chapters taken from the bible as well as paintings being changed and statues being stolen from Egypt, Greece, and Rome? Why were the Indians robbed of this very same land that we live on and claimed it was discovered by Christopher Columbus and renamed? Why do we celebrate holidays that were made up from stolen history? Why was the Sabbath moved from Saturday to Sunday? Why was and is Christmas celebrated on the winter solstice as the birth of Jesus Christ when he was actually born in the spring and placed in a manger? There are many questions that we as the western people of the world don't ask. If we do ask, we are terrorist and people that are a part of cults and rebelling. What was set up for us to follow, but it was set up to keep us dumb, deaf, and blind to what is really going on and what needs to be done as a whole. What was the war between the Confederates and the Union, that was based on the 13 colonies and led by General George Washington, about? Who I might say was a Freemason.

History does not repeat itself. It is rewritten. Styles are repeated. The first president of this country was proclaimed the United States was John Hanson under the Confederacy. History is rewritten for a reason. So the truth will not be told; the teachings that they don't teach you in history class. We speak about the Vatican; the war between the Muslims and the Catholics. What about the war on the homeless? The war on hunger? The war on diseases that has not been cured? You have to save the all mighty dollar to be in the races of anything.

Chapter 11
Poverty. Modern Slavery.

Many issues never get resolved but only forgotten about. We really don't know what poverty is until we go to another country in the Middle East and beyond. We have dealt with black slavery when slavery has been going on in other countries for centuries. We speak about how the law is not harsh enough until we hear how people are stoned to death because of a crime they have committed. We speak about how bad it is inside of the prison system, but yet tend to forget how it is in Mexico and other countries. Their conditions are worse, from hygiene, starvation, and inhumanity.

We are accustomed to a lifestyle where we do what we please, inside of the guidelines of the Constitution and we are spoiled because of the First Amendment. We have it easy compared to other countries outside of ours but complain that we don't get our way or not enough. The cost of living is expensive at times, but if we take a look at those across seas and see that they struggle just to maintain let alone elevate to any other level. Although poverty is rising they as a people appreciate more and feel blessed to what they have and do thank God for life.

I am not saying crime does not reside in other countries. Chopping a person's hand off is justice in some countries, but the enjoyment of waking up is still a blessing. We take life for granted.

We take advantage of things and do not appreciate and what we are blessed with. We complain about loud music. We complain about what's not being given to us. We complain about injustice. What do we do about all of this? Not much or even anything at all. We sit back and drink away our sorrows. We lay back and do drugs to escape things. We cheer and congratulate the wrong doers. We are so caught up in our own ways and actions we don't look at what is right around us and participate in keeping it alive.

Instead, we promote madness. We promote violence. We teach our children to fire weapons and wonder why their generation acts the way they do. We need more programs. More parents with children events. More sports events and activities that promote positive appearances and actions from the suburbia neighborhoods to the urban life.

We instead look at the monster that we don't understand, fear it, and commit to throwing punches at it. Come out with laws such as "stand your ground" and abuse the whole essence of its nature. Some of us don't even know what our talents are. We grow old and don't even know our purpose or destination in life. Finding ourselves is far from the lifestyle we are trying to uphold or the fact that we are brainwashed to just work, pay bills, and just stay afloat.

In the midst of this, the media shows how violence and rage are conquering the world and we as a people need to unite and take care of what someone else feels; as though it is wrong.

World bullies. We gain money for war which puts us into debt economically but we don't see it until the damage is done.

Chapter 12
Thoughts on Legacy

What about the legacy we leave? When the war is over. When the battle is on our own lawns, people sometimes blame the parents for the actions of the child, but not looking at what the child was watching or being taught by society and not the parent.

Our actions always catch the eye of the child. We feel as though since they are children we don't have to explain anything to them and don't owe them any explanation, but in fact, they are absorbing what is right and the wrong and coming up with their own conclusion.

Knowledge is knowing and having that knowledge creates wisdom. You have the words of a wise person that manifests the understanding of one's thoughts. With knowing the words; knowing changes the manifested wisdom into understanding.

It can be taught easily for our future, so order and loyalty can be brought to light. People say we are born to die, but between the beginning and the end, so much can be learned, taught, and practiced to carry on with honor and truth.

I speak about legacies. I speak about fallen warriors. I speak about teachings that go all the way back to Hermes Trismegistus.

All are sometimes forgotten. Speeches were spoken for reasons. Debates were argued for equality and battles were fought for justice. The circle of life was created to keep the balance of nature at ease. To keep all human races equal. To keep animals at peace. To have laws of nature repeated and followed by all. Humans were not created to be perfect, but that's not to say we do not strive for perfection. No one's life is the same, and their obstacles are different and handled differently. Regardless, whatever the problem, it can be fixed or made right without frustration or anger. When anger becomes involved we lose sight of how to handle it and the means of handling it is harsh.

Look at past history, starting with the Watts riots in "1965". Yes a vicious crime was committed intentionally and a trial was held, and a not guilty plea was announced. The reaction was unspeakable. For every cause, there is a reaction. It was a racial crime. It spread throughout the country. It mainly took place in California where the crimes mainly took place. This type of racism lived in those times everywhere. Certain races, under law or not, were the victims and justice was seriously blind.

The law was the accusers. It intended to slow down the violence, because of world leaders who only expressed love, peace, and by any means necessary. All had the goal of peace, freedom, and equality; and then to be hit again in the media in the year "1992" with the Rodney King beating.

That once again fueled an already angry race with the brutal assaulting of someone from another nationality, and again a trial took place, and the verdict was handed down from the jury of our peers, as a not guilty verdict.

Once again action and reaction, cause and effect, riot's occurred but this time things were different. All of our leaders who spoke freely about peace, equality, and freedom were kicked in the faces with the injustice of man's laws.

"No justice. No peace!" became the words of a nation that was in an uproar of the madness and pain which would be felt throughout our country. The desire for equality became greater amongst the intended race, and the reaction was violence.

What we knew was wrong felt right, because what we knew was wrong at those times was right to the accusers. We say two wrongs don't make a right but we will be even. Truth be told, karma has a way of talking to us. Good and bad. Sometimes that energy we see; we can only feel and hear when the wind blows hard. It's in every living thing. It is in matter, but we call it anti-matter. Even the least of us believe in anti-matter. Some call it the higher being. Some call it God. Some call it Allah and others call it Buddha.

All we know is that the unpredictable and the most divine being, thing, or energy ever known is man. We have the laws of nature, let alone the Ten Commandments handed down by Moses.

In reality, there were more. The truth has to continuously be told for the sake of mankind. We speak of valor and courage but forget about the whole truth. It has to be applied to the foundation which we build our temple, and on the principles set down for us.

Where we as people get our principles from? It starts with the morals and the respect that our parents instill in us as children. From then on life's experiences come into play.

Chapter 13
Live and learn.

Growth and Development. Teachings and Philosophies. Rules and Regulations. Long-Term and Short-Term Goals. Achievements and Rewards. Wins and Loses. All these things come from the experiences of living life. It has been said life is what we make it. But, what happens when a path is chosen for us that we have to live and it's not really the life that we want to live? For example marriages that are set up all because a person has their own intentions, instead of thinking of the next person's interest. We sometimes accept things because it makes others happy, saying what about my life? We don't make it; we just accept it. Some deal with it and some live miserably, but as I said before, everybody has his/her own purpose and is needed by someone.

If you don't like your status, change it. If you don't like the road you are traveling on, re-route. Everything starts within self first. Whatever is not right with nature and understanding of yourself, put your faith in God or your higher being or your choice, and take one step at a time. First, desert what you once knew and rebuild on principles that manifest some type of understanding and apply it to your everyday life. Whatever is not right with your nature and what you understand yourself to be, as well as, choose the right path. Things will fall into place. Things will start to work for you quietly. We cannot change what's not broken. Your faith keeps you strong and your will power keeps you going and what you gain along your path keeps you striving for more. We have to create our own laws for our own journey. It helps keep us in line. We are the rulers of our own destination, the kings, and queens of our own kingdom.

You are the pharaohs of your temple. You are the king of Greece. You are the conqueror of Rome. The teacher within your home. You are the controller of your own mind. You are the only one that can break your own mold. Getting back to what you once destroyed is a great accomplishment.

It weighs more because it comes from within. We have a more meaningful cause; logic and reason, goals and accomplishments, and conscience and subconscious thoughts. We start asking why to the mirror of answers. What we get back is the truth, but it all goes to the correction of the home we have built.

The way we move and the way we speak. All starts with a thought. They say a negative thought is not a sin unless it gets put into play or if you dwell on it for too long. The battle between good and evil will always be. It was started in the beginning. Who started it is always the question. The truth is always bold and has its own way of coming to the light. Even when smoke screens arise through manipulation and deception. The truth shines through dark shaded areas and even when the storm is catastrophic. The truth always comes out.

Some are still waiting for the truth to come about the government and the conspiracies. The "Jason Society" are scientific groups set up to run different parts of the whole world take over. Just like the Vatican is a cover up for the "Friendly Society".

During the assassination of John F. Kennedy, it was presented that the driver shot him. Why wasn't that put into the media? It was in many lectures but died out over time. How about the planting of the HIV/AIDS virus to specific nationalities to kill off the overpopulated world. The fact that we are still wondering if aliens landed here from outer space, even though there is proof, as well as, many other sightings.

We know the weapon named "Excalibur" was created to kill off any alien life form that has a weapon that can kill us off. Did man really walk on the moon and if so what was the government's whole intentions? Why did the American people want a female in office as President? Why are we not allowed in Area 51? Why can't we climb Mt. Everest unless we are some kind of government official with a particular clearance?

We put our trust in the same people who pull the wool over our eyes and deceive us with lies and false hope. Why are we allowed to protest but when they, meaning law enforcement, say it's over they began to pull out and cuffs and threaten to lock us up to close the mouths of the voices that can reach far distances?

Why was Arnold Schwarzenegger, who was a movie actor, able to win the election as governor and still go back into acting once his term was over? We also know he is from the black family of England. Why did George H. W. Bush as the Director of the CIA allow drug smuggling but arrested those who did the same thing.

Is it because we don't pay taxes for something that is illegal or is it because they allow us to sell the drugs which give them a job as Law enforcement agents to lock us up? Why did J. P. Morgan, David Rockefeller, Rothschild and a few other guys make the

Federal Reserves banking anyway?

Is all of this a test or is it a game to keep the power in the hands of the wealthy? Is it a pleasure to keep the American people blind from the true reason or a pain knowing we are getting tricked up knowledge thrown at us every time we begin to get a little rest and turn on the tunes?

Every day is different. Every moment is not the same. If you were to keep God in your life and not worry about how you will make it from one point to another, things would come a little easier. You may not worry about how you will handle them.

Life is based on choices. You will make the right one or you make the wrong one. The right one you get a stepping stone forward while the wrong one you get a step backward. Life is about the pursuit of happiness that's why people look for love because it makes them happy.

Money is not a root of evil. People want it so much because it makes things a little easier dealing with bills and experiences. It comes with greed, one of the devils, not the five; jealousy, envy, lust, envy, and hate. The more things that come into your grasp and more obstacles only heighten the moment of victory as you overcome those things with true meaning.

We all want the greater things in life. We want them the easy way knowing certain things are harder to accomplish. Some things we achieve and some things we don't get the chance to even try, but life goes on with or without us in it.

We live and we learn. Life's experience right? We just have to look at things from a greater perspective and take them for what they are worth and make the most of them.

Chapter 14
Assets, Liabilities,
And Investments

Now let's talk about assets and liabilities. Assets are material things that we may own but pay taxes on them annually. It's collateral if you ever need a loan or assistance as far as a cash flow. As long as we pay taxes on it, it's partially yours and the bank or your city owns it. It's actually government property that is being taken care by you and being profited by the government. We can register it, and profit off of it ourselves, or just reside in it as our home. We may never actually own it.

Now liability is an investment that is in your name. Investment is constantly flipping money and building interest as years go on. You may invest in a bank, but the bank uses your money to invest into other things. You are actually investing in the economic system that keeps the stock market balanced. Now it may be a good thing because it is less money coming out of your pocket to pay for anything. Your investment is paying for ownership of any property that you own. It starts with an idea, a thought, or an action, then an accomplishment.

Even then the ball doesn't stop rolling. We want more so we have to achieve more. Yes, the times may be harder than some, but we can't let it discourage us from our goals. We can't let it discourage us from the initial idea. We can't let it discourage us from what we must accomplish to get to the end of the road. Only to starts over again, but better. Stay focused.

There are many programs out there with job offerings, but in order to know it, you have to be in that trend. That trend of wanting more in life and know what you have to do to get it. No cutting corners. No slacking off. No sleeping late and no missing days. Get it by any means. Everyone gets one chance. Everyone has that one time to shine. In the words of a famous artist, "You better lose yourself in the music the moment you own it, you better not never let go, you only get one shot, do not miss your chance to blow, this opportunity comes once in a lifetime."

Never look back because it is only darkness behind you. Never look back with regrets or failure. If we don't fall how will we know what getting up feels like? How do we know what winning is if we don't lose? Every failure is an experience in what not to do, let alone what to do. It helps us know what it feels like, what the bottom is and what we have to do to stay on the top or just winning. What we can't win every time we play the game of life, but it's a passion of wanting to win knowing your chances are to lose. Some days may be easier than others depending on what your goal for that day, but we still must go hard. Go hard like it's your last time like it's your last breath, or like it's your last day.

Never give up because you can't see the end. Never give up when a problem arrives. Never give up because you think you can't push anymore. That's when things get better. You get more focused. You get more accurate. One false move you can lose the game so you bob and weave and roll with the punches that are being thrown at you knowing the fight will be over soon. The bell will ring any minute.

Now let me touch on this thing that everybody does not like to speak about, but it does exist.

Chapter 15
Racism

Yes, Martin said, "We shall overcome someday." Yes, the hippies said, "Just have fun and it's about peace." But in all actuality, it exists in many races of people now as it did then. Yes, the Jewish Holocaust is over, but the Germans still feel they are the superior race. Yes, Abraham Lincoln freed the slaves, but slavery still went on, yet no longer visible today.

Did you know there were 13 Presidents who owned slaves and we are taught to respect them as equals? People still deal with white supremacy and feel as though their race is superior to what we know as the black race. The black race was called vicious names and was considered nothing but savages. Wow. These things may not exist anymore but they do in the minds of a few.

Even in Florida with the vigilante "Stand your Ground Law" is even being taken advantage of due to the racism that is in the minds of others but they call it being prejudice. We are still stuck on false images that have been painted to display white faces replacing black images. Rewriting history and taking out the accomplishments of Blacks and Jews.

The painting of Jesus and the Virgin Mary are only replicas of the statues and story of Horus and the Virgin Mother Isis. The races were changed to display them white. The "Statue of

Liberty" was changed from a woman out of slavery with cut shackles to a woman holding a torch that stood for Independence. Even religions that we believe in today as false statements have been rewritten to suit the ears of the so-called superior race. All teachings and methods that we believe in this current day started in Egypt or Ethiopia. The pyramids were raided by Alexander the Great accompanied by Aristotle, The Greeks, Hebrews, and other thieves. Plato, Socrates, Aristotle, Jesus, Moses, and many other well-known famous people of history went to the schools in Egypt where the most highest priest was teaching inside the temple. They taught the Egyptian mystery system, magic, many secrets and rites that are no longer taught today.

Egyptians are the mothers and fathers of almost all the Greek gods, Astronomy, Astrology, Geometry, the Correct Calendar, and many other scientific methods of dealing with life.

Chapter 16
Black Facts.

The Ten Commandments that were handed down by Moses, the lawgivers, are all from the original forty-two (42) Negative Confessions by Egypt. The beginning of civilization was dark-skinned people; actual Black facts. The white race did not want to feel inferior to the blacks so a plan came about. Get rid of them and the history and make up their own which would make sense being as though it was the Egyptian truth from the beginning.

It is America that we praise and love. The home of the free and the land of the brave, so they say. We are never free but brave. We are never equal but bleed the same. No race is superior or inferior to the other. Not whites. Not blacks. Not Jews. No religion is better than the other. Not Christianity. Not Islam. Not Buddhism. Not Judaism. All are ways of life that lead to the Supreme Being most of us believe in. Just different ways of studying it.

People even downgrade science. It is evolution which can explain things from animal to man, but not from monkeys. Was it from the Big Bang Theory that gave us the ability to evolve from water, we don't know. We would never know the whole truth about the beginning. What we don't understand, we come up with a hypothesis and make it seem right to the naked eye and ear, then it comes into birth. Then the belief is driven by fear and applied through man because of its teachings.

Mathematics is the law which comes with understanding. The Egyptian Mystery System and reading of hieroglyphics can help us understand how things came into play as far as one Dynasty to the next and futuristic became the modern life. We even have atheist who believe that we were accidents.

Wow. Not believing in higher energy that can be seen (anti-matter) nor heard but can be felt in everything and can be expressed in things that come with nature as a little mysterious. Nature gives birth to all and its father can only be felt not seen. Life will always keep us guessing. The smarter we get, the more interesting things become. We discover more and more.

From microscopes to telescopes. From Hypothesis to the truth. It's the fact of not knowing that keeps us guessing and wanting to know more. This is the beauty of life. Just like a male to a female. We would never quite understand a woman and we may pass with still never knowing the woman but it's the beauty of finding out.

Interesting.

Chapter 17
Mother Nature and the Woman

Mother Nature and the woman are the whole reproductive system of living things. Man and the Supreme Being are the en-lighteners and the fathers of what Mother Nature and the woman conceive and which comes into existence. Nature is really never tampered with. It has its own laws and its own way of shaping and fertilizing what we know to be plant life forms. With the help of the wind, water, earth, and many other atoms, molecules, protons, neutron, and electrons, plant life is fertilized. The four seasons are examples how things grow and die. At certain times of the year, plant lifeforms reproduce and are brought back to life even more and better than before.

The mother carries fluids to her child through the belt and sack that the child is growing in and the blood helps to keep protein and other vitamins flowing to the child. Then the woman has the strength to push the child out, and the life is born so everyone can see.

Without Mother Nature and the mother of the children, no life will be produced. Men are the controllers of whether life exists inside of the woman. Just like without the sun, there would be no air there would be no human, plant, or animal life form. Men are the en-lighteners of life that are reproduced by the woman.

Men are not sole contributors of human life. Men help teach the minds and the growth of the child. We defend and protect the woman and child with our own life, as well as, provide for the family. The woman also helps mold and shape the child.

It's not complicated, just a mystery. It's like I said before, knowledge is beyond our understanding. There's more left to the universe than this galaxy we live in. Even the story of human anatomy is a mystery. We all know from health class in high school that a bone is a mineralized tissue. It gives great tactile strength for the tendons, which attaches to the muscle, as well as, the ligaments which attach the bones together at the joints. We were also taught that blood is a liquid of plasma containing salt, water, and proteins. It represents the red blood cells and is for the immune system. The heart keeps the blood pumping throughout the body. Without the heart, the body shuts down. If a disease is caught within the body, the bloodstream carries it from one part of the body to another. The blood cells help prevent infections throughout the body.

The body is energized with vitamins and proteins. Exercise keeps the molecules in shape because of the aging. Obesity is a problem. It causes unwanted conditions in the body which are unhealthy and can cause clogged arteries, high blood pressure and any other things that lead to heart attacks or strokes.

Chapter 18
Beliefs From Within And Without

But we must always keep faith in a higher being, or energy if not very religious, and never resent yourself or past actions. The energy that we look for is within one's self.

The Hindu believes in a Supreme Being, the Braham, who is uncreated, unborn, changeless, and divine holy. They believe that the holy one is within all of us, and the ability to believe is in us all. What we do with it is up to us.

We must know and understand what we dish out is what we get back. We will never understand the mysteries of the world or the way nature moves, but knowing ourselves is a power that we possess. We have powers we are born with. We lose our focus because of what we are taught through our parents, radio, media, movies, and even cartoons.

Illuminati is everywhere but we just don't notice it. CBS, back of the dollar bill, Rap and R&B artist, police force, correction facilities, banks, Trilateral Commission, Council of Foreign Relations, Skull & Bones, Bilderberg Society, Freemasons, some of the Presidents who signed the Constitution of Amendments. The list goes on and on. We just cannot be closed minded to everything just because it doesn't sound like the path we were used to seeing or being taught to believe. Ignorance runs far but some don't know how ignorant they are until presented with the truth.

But when the truth flies in our face and through our ears, will we accept it or deny it? Will we research it or will we just close the book? I've seen people glance at a few passages in books and turn them away because it is not things they were use to reading or hearing.

The Western religion and way of life have its hold on us and our children to where we don't want to see a separate path to the divine. Take science for example. It gives us many answers to a lot of questions that we ask, but don't get it in our religion. Some call it the devil or an untold way of following things as far as looking for answers. Christianity their God says if you ask questions it shows rebelliousness and it's a sin. That means you will always be blind to things and questions that you may have or will never be answered because it wasn't meant to be answered. That sounds like a man-made thing if you ask me.

A way to tell the people that they don't know. Truth is everywhere. You just have to seek it. It has been said, "seek and you shall find." Even in cartoons. So why is it a sin to have questions that will only complete your path to knowledge? As I said before, knowledge is beyond infinite. We are still trying to figure out how our bodies co-exist with the universe. Why do we as young males wake up to an erection in the morning when the sun comes up? Why are we born in a certain zodiac we have specific suns and we act a specific way when that time of the year comes. There are many questions we ask and science gives us some answers, and others will never be answered.

Chapter 19
A Journey of Experience
And Knowledge.

A mystery. Skeptical but amazing. A journey of trials and tribulations. A journey of mysteries and amazement. You can discover new things on how to go about handling life every day you live it; its ugliness, its beauty, its glory, and its cycle. We may ask ourselves what happens to the energy in which some call it the spirit after the physical forms can no longer function.

Some say go to heaven or hell depending on how you lived it and others like the Hindus believe in the karma-marga which states, "If a murder committed in one's life may cause the murderer to be murdered himself in the next." A life of selfishness may result in the next being filled with preservation and loneliness. This is what is meant by "karma"; the Law of Cause and Effect.

In modern life, we think that what we do, just because it is not seen by the naked eye, it is not seen at all. We are getting away with it. Not believing in good or bad karma. The cosmic laws of the universe teach us to understand the laws of nature in which it was produced to follow so no chaos, destruction, or misunderstanding can be made due to not knowing and corruption. Sins are noticed and they do not go unanswered or undetected. The Eastern Religion and philosophies are totally different from the way the Westerners study religion.

Christianity that we study today is rewritten and translated in many ways and the words of the Bible are either taken out or added in; as well as Islam. All the words that are written in Hebrew or Greek cannot be translated in English or Arabic. We would have to actually know the language to understand it better and even if so we would never find or let alone look at the original translations.

We do not know how to read hieroglyphics. So we do not know what's on the pyramids. We may attend school to study different languages to help us figure things out. But, once we know these things, we'll find out that what western civilization has been taught is false, and based on someone else's understanding.

What will we do with the truth? The Catholic Pope is still apologizing for what was said and taught in the past. The Catholic Church had a big influence in changing the words in the Bible and plays a part in the war that has been going on for centuries between other religions and the Illuminati, whose web worldwide influences scientist in Switzerland, and in the ways of life from east to west.

There are some, who have a different point of views, acting badly toward people whose opinions are different from theirs, and they choose not to open their minds and consider the information could possibly be true. This is due to their way of life or religion, which tells them that if you are studying or following other religions other than that one, you will go to hell because it is a sin. In all actuality, there were many people who lived their life and they worshiped many gods millions of years ago speaking different languages.

The modern day religion is the replica of those ways of living and practices. We get mad at the people who study Satanism and say that they will definitely go to hell. Why? If I'm right, Lucifer is not only God's best angel, but the name means 'the bringer of light'. He has to be respected.

So the bible says. So is it that the bringer of light is also telling the truth and his punishment out of heaven was only because he disobeyed? He was cast onto Earth as well as his followers, 1/3 of the angels. Others who believe he was right to a certain extent. Hell is only an image given by those who want the Bible to be true. They want to plant in the minds of its readers fear and they would have no choice but to follow what is written and have more followers; more domination.

Is it true that God would punish those who are not saved and have them put into a pit that they will burn for all eternity? That doesn't sound like a nice God. But we are all born sinners and neither man nor woman is perfect. Even Thomas Jefferson attempted to rewrite the bible or did he?

When will we open our own minds and not doubt what we are taught, and also not deny what is different? Every man and woman are different and we accept them as they are. So why not accept their different ways of life?

In Confucianism, it pays honor to the human person and to the society we create. It honors the idea of balance and harmony. He believed that creating peace, living harmoniously, and cultivating society is the highest goal we can achieve in life.

This way of life and his teachings are not practiced over here in the western civilization or in our modern day living. We are so busy worrying about what a person is saying and not saying; doing and not doing. We criticize what their actions are instead of just pointing out flaws that are seen but they cannot see in themselves with their own eyes.

Even so, people still cannot take constructive criticism. They think the person is dealing with jealousy or hate and trying to be persecuted so they react in a way of violence because of misunderstandings. Peace and love start from within.

You would think as one gets older, they would know this and express it. It can be taught to one another or as well as tolerance. We take it and set standards for our own self. We talk about those who did not get it yet, instead of stepping up and being a leader. We are outside of our masters and we bite the hand that feeds us. We talk down those who have low self-esteem to make ourselves feel good. To make ourselves feel superior to those who we are weaker than we are.

One is lost because of the path they were once led to believe is true. A path that was once taught to believe it was the way out. A path that was once preached about to understand that it was the way to a saved heart and to heaven.

We compromise. Instead of making one feel like home is secure and safe, and when once we step away, the door locks are changed, the windows are barricaded and no one knows you anymore. The wilderness is a cold place to be with nobody along side of you. No place to rest the body of all health and parasites and cleanse the soul of all evilness and where confessions are forgiven.

Chapter 20
Taking Action.

There are different demons of all sorts of creatures. Some God created, and some are soul takers. They are bottom dwellers along with the creatures of the sea. The monsters in the closet and monsters under the bed. Evil always lurks somewhere, but without evil, we would not know how it feels to do good or feel joy, to feel sorrow or pain.

We just watch the path that we take and look out for the wicked witch of the West or East…North and South. Know she has associates to help the negative souls succeed for their own comfort, for their own illusions. Some souls never rest or are just stuck in what people call the tunnel of light.

Why? We will never really know. We say how much we love life and the joy it brings, but cannot establish unity amongst ourselves; let alone our own community. So how can we enjoy any happiness with the fear of humiliation, by other's actions, even though it is not us as individuals causing the disunity?

Then we wonder why some communities are stronger than others. Why some communities are cleaner and have more programs and activities more than the others. Why? Simply because of unity. It means a lot. We overcome oppression and destruction because of unity. We as a nation have won wars because of unity and nations are still together because of unity. No secrets are told and no bridges are crossed. No infiltration and no chaos come from unity. Understanding principles of human life. "If we don't stand for something we fall for anything."

Unity! We defy it and at the same time, we go against it. Within our own country, we turn against each other. We can't stop the violence even though some establish peace rallies. Even though some of our forefathers fought and died for peace. Still, there's no unity. No balance. No peace. No progress.

We have killings in elementary schools. We have states like Georgia who lead in massive building bombings. We are still curious about how the World Trade Center fell along with a building that was not hit.

Do we blame our government for that who killed countless people? Just a thought. What about the Oklahoma City bombing? How about the Kennedy assassination? What about the Watts riots? What are they still saying about hurricane Katrina? Where was FEMA?

I can go on and on about how our own country does not stand for unity amongst our own people; let along forming unity against other countries that don't like what we are doing to them. The media never tells the entire story and we still believe them. They look at us like we are the terrorist. And we have all sorts of names for those who don't like us as Americans and the democracy.

On the other hand, we are accepted by some and appreciated by others. Unity starts from the love within them to others. It overrides all evil and pushes back against the oppressor without even one act of violence or threat. Everything is a test. Why? Only those who make it know the real reason. Why? Domination.

We can't even control our own forefront let alone another country that has inner program "Focus." Focus is the key to keeping your head on the official road. Focus. It may not have your vision seeing beyond your intended target. Focus. It may have your mind cloudy with negative judgment because of haters or jealousy that comes from those who would not like to see you make it because you're making it weakens their superiority ego "Drive." Drive is the speed in which you are taking to achieve your goal of accomplishments. Drive. It is the motivation that keeps you energized with statements like, "I can do it or I can make it happen regardless of what's in my way. I can."

I can are those words you say when you think times are getting in the way. "I can" will always fuel that drive. "I can" will always recharge that focus when feeling blurry. That feeling in which the mountain you are climbing is getting steeper. You always must know every road is not easy. It gets worse before it gets better. The road becomes smoother and shorter, easier to accomplish. Just staying afloat is work that has to always be done.

It's even harder to do without family support, with financial problems, and being the average person who is on the outside looking in. They don't understand why you are doing what you are doing, let alone what you have been through to get to the point you are at. People will talk about you regardless of what you are doing, whether it be right or wrong. Whether it be good or evil. Whether it be for charity. You could never do enough to fulfill everyone's pleasure. That is why you have to please yourself first, family next and others who love you after.

Never be ashamed to say, "No." Never be afraid to go against the opposition. Never be afraid to shine as bright as you can. Just for the day express how much you want freedom and equality throughout your community, even though freedom is not really free. Just for the day read an extra chapter or two in your favorite book. Just for the day you lay down your weapons and walk the streets freely. Just for the day, say to yourself you will not lose. Just think, we will one day look at things at an old age and consider our old mistakes and wonder why we did them in the first place.

Never stop believing. Never stop climbing. Never stop seeking the truth for it is out there. Never become closed minded because someone or thing told you to be. Never stop learning, for new things are being rediscovered. Never stop striving for perfection, for divinity is within us. Never stop glorifying the almighty, for it is the holiest or holies. Never stop elevating the mind, for maintaining is stagnation. Never stop reaching for the sky, for the stars can be touched. Never stop surfing the waves, for the ocean is another beautiful creation of nature. Never stop dancing, because the music will always play. Never take a day off for the struggle still continues, and never stop loving, because it is the deepest emotion of all.

Just open your eyes and see the future is near. Never close your ears for the truth will always be taught to the open-minded individual who wants to learn and carry on the practices and rests from the past. Never allow pride or ego stand in the way of balance and peace. We can learn something new every day. Just never be close minded.

What the world, well western style of things, wants to believe is only half truth, and the rest is one's own understanding of the truth or what they want it to be perceived. Just like American history. In order to learn more after high school, schooling has to be paid for. Knowledge cost money and in wanting it you lose nothing.

If you do not have a 4.0-grade average, nobody will pay for schooling for you. So you either have to get a low-income job just to make it or do what you have to just to make it, or do what you have to pay for it yourself and your degree. It's an investment for those who have it.

At this day and age we now live in, technology took over everything. It makes it easier to learn, but even then you still have to pay for certain knowledge set in books we may come across on the Internet.

It's a modern day black market here in America. The Internet is something that the government can control. In America, it is thought if you are not a good investment, you have to settle for less. Don't worry about getting a higher education; it's only for the bright. Who's to say you are not that bright one? Who's to say you are not the next physician or lawyer if given a chance at life? You could be the best you could be.

In order to be highly successful in life, it starts with schooling, which is free up until high school. Anything more than the high school you have to pay.

An eye is kept on our everyday phone calls. There are actually people who get paid to watch those who are on a special list. This list was created for those who may have rebelled against the system. It was created to keep them classified because they tried to bring to the truth, and now they are labeled.

Chapter 21
Modern World View.

We are afraid to speak against the system, because of the assassinations of the best, and because leaders have been put away. It exists. They set the standards. They want stability as they see it to never be broken. They want to silence the voice that everyone hears. They only let a few words pass because some may not read anyway.

Now let's briefly speak of the faith of someone's religion. We must note that religion is only understood as divine being. No one will actually know how or what created us as humans let alone animals or any other kind of species. But we do know science can show specific things and religion is mainly hearsay.

There are so many ways to study Islam and many ways of looking at Christianity which is cut up into many different classes which take us into heaven.

One religion is at war with the other but both contradict each other until you read them in its original form. How anyone who reads them in the English language says it is right and properly understand them? You have some that still believe and worship deities, and others say they are wrong and are cults. Until we learn Greek, Arabic, or Latin we are not going to know if we are right.

The battle will always be fought. The paths are the same, just different languages. In trying to understand the different ways to practice, we are still confused and even when science comes into play, both concepts battle against each other about who is right and who is wrong.

No modern western way of life is wrong (a lie) but only half right (true). It's our faith that keeps teaching, rites, ceremonies, and practices alive. It's that we believe the reason why we sing. We sing because we praise the almighty. We sing to give testimony to what we have witnessed or seen. We sing because miracles are answered. We sing to emphasize our right to protect. We sing to hold up our rights against our accusers. We sing to let our voices be heard by the gods.

We must never abandon hope because we believe in something. We must never abandon hope because we want change. We must never abandon hope because change will come. We must never abandon hope because some need help due to voices that were silenced because of age. We must never abandon hope because we have been going on hope for years. We must never abandon hope because our children always need a better future and something to hold on to.

Chapter 22
Truth in Communications.

Silence is never useful. It can be heard. It is only seen when actions speak louder than words. Words carry into our future and can be heard amongst millions. Silence can sometimes win a battle because saying close to nothing can keep a person curious. It can make a person back away because they may not know how to take the other person.

At the same token silence can be damaging because that voice could change the nation. That voice could encourage those who are in the nation. That voice could be the word heard across the world. That voice could be the sound that moves the crowd. That voice could be the sound of a perfect song and that voice could be the sound to awaken a person from a deep slumber.

One voice. One sound. One movement. One love. It is said intelligence is a gift, not a right. Knowledge is an only logical reason to a problem that surfaces amongst the people of society. This means understanding is the ultimate goal to one's conflict? So correct the lack of understanding that comes from ignorance, eliminate misunderstanding and bring forth the truth.

Without the truth, we would be lost. Without the truth, negativity would prevail. Truth makes us understand the misunderstood. Truth makes us free from the ultimate slavery of the mind trapped in a state of disbelief. Truth makes us wise and makes us speak with words of wisdom. Truth makes us strong and well prepared for the battle we may be facing. Truth is the key to one's destination, and truth makes us indivisible against the trick knowledge that we are brainwashed with daily.

As long as we look for the truth we may never be blinded from the facts that open our ears, eyes, and mind which craves for that sight of hope and happiness. It opens us up to that joy that makes us smile; and that laughter that we feel in us when we feel love and emotions. It opens us up to that courage when we need to stand tall and that fire that burns non-stop in the pilot each evening in the midst of slumber.

We all need a helping hand and at the same time, we must lend a hand. 'One hand washes the other' and both wash the face as people tend to show. Many follow those very words that seem so easy to do. We say the rich stay rich by only giving and helping those that are not wealthy.

What about those who don't have the ability to make it because of financial issues, but have potential to succeed? Do we wash their hands with our hands and pull that person one step closer to their goal? Or do we make fun of the person because they don't have what we have, and talk badly about them to our likings? Is this the process of 'keeping a good man down' or is it being taught by the rich? Or is it just slavery of the mind they want you to stay in because of superiority?

Ego. There is no self-righteousness behind the madness. There is no self-righteousness behind sickness. Purity is developed by repenting and cleansing of the body. Let's say we are born angels, but once we are taught that we have the ability to judge right and wrong and choosing between the two, we become sinners of the flesh. But, only God can judge us. Choices are judged with the opinion of others. Being judgmental is false (wrong).

That's when these four devils come into play; Denial and misinterpretation; Prosecution and crucifixion. Remembering at the end of the day exercising perfection is a must. The energy that revolves around you and the energy it attracts helps push off bad rubbish. Be positive, have an aura of positive practices, positive people and things around you that are successful.

We need to have the desire and our hunger for goals to be achieved, to be based on will power. We need to be leaders with inspiration, with the external strength to overcome competition; with the intent to win. We need the proper education, street knowledge, dedication, and self-control knowing anything is possible.

You plan for success and the pleasure you get is peace of mind which your family gets when you are the coach of the team. Being proud of your achievement encourages you to do more. It is the great feeling you get when you receive stimulation from being the speaker, a positive role model, an optimist, and an extremist.

You are the good messenger with supernatural wisdom. Heaven is within a halo over your head. Innocence protects you from chaos with the kind of wings that are angelic as they say.

Invisible. Triumph over madness and the spiritual being of a God. Miracles do happen that cannot be explained. With the divine creator and the music of a beautiful song, you become holy for all eternity. Crowned with the form that is painted with a pure messenger of knowledge and information that may be filled with symbols and language of the ancient writers. You must move the line a fraction in which it can be written, printed, and published for all can see, read, and hear.

Understand this, the truth must be written in all languages based on numerous topics with volumes that range from childhood to old age. Many series and subjects must be explained by authors of books or voices heard across a microphone. Facts can be researched online on pages written by man about science, about the past or present events; from many editions of a dictionary, many categories in a library; and many articles printed in a bibliography. Information from these sources that have been told must be heard.

Truth has to be written in easy to read content so all can understand. In text written for the ignorant, let it be understood instead of judged or criticized. Know this, an ignorant person will be against what is being said because their mind is shut and they feel as though what they already know is right. They always say, 'can't teach an old dog new tricks'. That's because the old dog doesn't want to be taught new tricks. It makes a person come out of their comfort zone and they no longer feel like a king or ruler of his own world.

The system is set up with laws and enforcement armies made to control and maintain penalties and activities for the policies have been set forth. Punishment in procedure and guidelines are the method of obedience. Safety of schools and neighborhoods can be managed with those accustomed to formal behavior. Not everybody has comprehension skills to catch everything one throws at him/her, but with truth explained in a way a child can understand and relate at times, it can break barriers that may have been built around the mind and the heart.

Houses were dedicated or governed with habits of a repetitive cycle. Doctrines are protected so they won't get into the hands of those who want to destroy them for the reasons of revealing truth. For instance, secrets that have been protected for years like the Holy Grail by the Knights Templars, which original names were "Order of the Poor Knights of Christ and the Temple of Solomon" were established by "The Priory of Scion" in 1099. They went through many battles and sacrifices with the Christians and the Catholic Churches and a few popes were in place to protect what was the truth. They protected what would reveal all, and what is made up by man and his religion and how they wiped out the truth, and replaced it with their own truth and called it the "religion" that we praise today?

Truth has been protected by covenants that have been taken and temples that have been raided and preventing our society to hear the truth became a secret because of the greed for power by past rulers, popes, kings, and priest. So in due respect to the fallen scientist, astronomers, alchemists, physician, and all their teachers, we must let the truth be in books, articles, TV, radio and all other sorts of things people find as entertainment and amusement. It's like being hypnotized into an altered state that has consequently come true with techniques of false hope thinking we will never make it and only attempting to produce magic in reality. Research, science, and studies have been performed to see if the subconscious mind can be controlled. If we have had dreams, been in dreams or never dreamt, can our reality be controlled by pain management, hypnotherapy, meditation because we think we don't have the strength to change?

People who want to have fun don't fit in. They will look at us like Satan or we are studying satanic rites because a good book that has been praised for years tells use otherwise. Influence with the threat of failing. Influenced into regression thinking we made one wrong step, even though our conscience is right. Now it's hard to quit smoking. Obesity is always a problem for the help and weight loss its inevitable awareness of the brain is weakened because over year loss faith the making of technologies where we don't need to use the whole brain all it is a press of a button and things work for us.

What is it that the devil told to convince the people that he doesn't exist? To get relief from sadness, rage, loneliness, grief, and guilt, all they need is confession and to repentance to make it easy to no longer feel the pain. Shame is no longer the object and a desire to be cheerful and develop peace starts within. Anger to be back on track where you once left off is the goal. Envy and living in horror doesn't cloud your judgment or movement. Pride lays aside and loves again. Realizing lust is a part of the five (5) devils. Depression is not in the heart or the soul and pleasure which pleases the mind. Pride is no longer the issue. We look for amusement, comedies, musicals, recreation and other activities that many restores and find freedom within their mind. Board games, card games, bowling, movies, sporting events, with the family all pertains to fun. Clowns and circus attractions become a part of the events and relaxation is at ease.

We look at television differently with the thoughts that may signal communities, with announcements that address the community, with broadcast information of the truth and inboxed worse codes, with an invitation to the ear and the mind to open and receive the truth. Emails, news or the media we have been explaining those will catch it and request encrypted or with words inspiring. Letters must be sent containing recordings of speeches that were once told and heard across as listeners of a change.

We have to take responsibility for our own actions and know change starts with self. Then we can put the word of our commitment out to our communities. We have to agree with our explanations, and how we couple the effect with a chance to change our local community hoping it would extend further. Opening opinions with votes that have terms with regulations that will overpower the war on crime. Government seats are up for positions for people who will supervise the town with political aspects. We need to fill chairs with those who are working toward the movement; managing executives, directors, secretaries, and councils. These people should all come with the purpose of guidance and leadership presentation with the help from people in high places and have the views as you do with support of a financial state.

Chapter 23
Truth Comes With Art.

Through years of televised programs, we looked closely through the lies that bore into our mind. These programs have been televised for years, and their replay will continue to be televised for years to come. The nations warred against each other. They lived for and cherished things that were made-up for us to believe is true. Nostradamus, Constantine, Socrates, King James, Leonardo Da Vinci, the Popes, Aristotle, and many others inspired those who shaped this nation to keep the truth hidden for the Roman churches sake. The Roman churches built this religion we call, Christianity.

Many schools have used their laboratories over and over again, to experiment and find how things were created. They focused on accumulating compounds, which are made up of structured substances, rather than create masses of matter, or solutions to problems that have fluids, hydrogen, oxygen, alchemy, and the basic study of chemistry.

They tried to find out how the Big Bang was started and what was created when matter and anti-matter were combined. They have been in search of elements that were created since the beginning of time. Equations are now being figured in metaphysics and carried on by new scientists rather in school or in Switzerland. Religion and science have each other. One is based on stories and the other is based on facts that can be visible today created or recreated.

We start with a children's encyclopedia which covers the basic of traditional, religion, creation, and many other subjects that may fit the interest of the child on figuring how things work. Encyclopedias for adults have history and science, and discoveries by famous inventors. It contains all things that people do not care to look at or it doesn't pertain to life and they cannot learn from it. As I said, ignorance runs far and they rather not notice the ignorance until a child comes up with a basic school question that they need help with and the adult cannot help them solve it. The child then looks at the adult and ponders with confusion. Who knows what runs through the mind of the adult?

Some have no hope and they choose not to look for a way out of the stages of ignorance and the famous statement is "Do not judge me." But in fact, the child is much smarter in education and wise until he/she makes their own decision to attend school or not. An adult is just a person who accepts the fact that their companion is not as bright as a bag of bricks, and they only can teach them about their life's experience, and could not help them with any educational project. Technology makes things easy. No longer do we have to open a book. No longer do we have to think about chaos, the computer does the work for you. People don't take the time out to learn about the computer. The computer does the work for you.

Sometimes the old school is better than the new school. All should be born with that drive to work and have that external strength to think. 'I think I can. I know I can' is the noise heard by the brain. 'I got to achieve something' is a deep feeling. 'Can't do it' is no longer in the vocabulary or the mind; and 'I can't stop, won't stop' becomes the language. The go-getting and working hard pays off. Either it is fast or slow it has to be done.

Stopping is failing. Failing is losing. You must get it by any means knowing the struggle will never stop but will ease up just a little only if you have the all mighty dollar. No one will be given things while others struggle just to get in the race. People don't love you when you don't have it and are by your side when you do have it. Separate the fake and the phony before you become original. Never forget the support you got when you were down and out. Remember the blessings you received and never take advantage of your blessings.

Don't forget where you came from and never lose focus of your path no matter how good it gets. Remember those who don't have and take care of those who love you unconditionally. When you do it, do it big. Do it so those can remember your name, legacy, and movement. They will remember your words, style, and language.

Always come with fury, but not frustration, knowing what is gained can be taken in an instant. Understand the movement and what has to be done. It has to be done with the heart of a lion. It only takes one step. Numbers are infinite. To get to our major goal it may take a while, but being on the path can be worth it. Fire has to be in the eyes and taste; the taste for blood has to be in the taste buds of the hungry.

No greed. Just thirsty desire to get what is owed to you so you can have success. Failure is enough drive or fuel for the journey. We have to just deal with patience knowing nothing is easy; ours or others. So never get depressed or stressed because of the fact of not having. Poverty is not what we think until we see poverty across seas. We see how others live. Some say they don't understand how it can be done or how they live in that way.

Adjustment is a must for those who do not know how it feels to not have. If all of what they have was taken, they could not be dealt with and suicide may result. The movie "Trading Places" was not aired for no reason, and I hope the lesson it taught has been caught by others.

People have to understand that winning is not everything and losing is part of the game or lesson. When and if you lose, try not to lose by much. Only points can keep hope alive and still be noticed and displayed as a winner. If you were to lose, know and understand there is always another time and using the time to overlook the mistakes made can only sharpen your strategy and better tactics can be used. The game still goes on and your presence can still be there by showing your support to the game itself if not having a chosen team.

You just have to maintain the mentality of a winner and know you can't win every time. Mother said it best, "If you do not let your friends win once, they will not come back and play again." All you have to do is win, no matter what it takes. Rock got knocked down and got back up more upset that he was better. More sustain. More incredible but as I said before winning is not everything; some fortunate…some less fortunate. Some get it and some just can't find it. Everyone still plays a part in this cage we call the world as we make it.

Chapter 24
Man's Laws and Commandments.

Policy and politics all deal with how a person networks. Your resources. Your intel. Your navigation. Your goal. Your ambition.

You have the fuel to travel at the speed of light. You have to know gravitational pull is not enough, and the distance to the cosmos. You have to know just in our solar system are many moons, stars, planets, suns, etc. let alone the universe itself. Now today we need spaceships using space technology that travels and orbits satellites NASA over, fusion or space or that haven't traveled out control. What happens when they come towards the direction of the planet? Astronomers know and understand these things along with geometry, music, and rhetoric. They understand data communications of the actions by the Trilateral Commission and other societies that can manipulate information passed down generation to generation, from family, and/or monitor and present it to our society, build other business whose secured surveillance is all secrecy. They have trained officers on 24/7 surveillance walking and patrolling with the purpose to contain areas that are visible to the naked eye. Their purpose of protecting is bigger than what we think.

The negative strategies with positive actions have been taken to keep the structure of power on them by creating jobs for certain groups and continue to penalize the ones who have broken the law or made simple mistakes which may cost him/her their freedom.

They may have been rehabilitated but still get patronized by the media or the society institutional until the war strikes home. Until their family member becomes the ones who is killed, nightmares become real.

Blackness no longer has a time. Ghosts and hooting from owls are heard throughout the day. Dreams turn to dusk and warmth turns to cold. They're on our doorstep. The monster will howl at the blackness filled with crickets and other creepy noises. Days become evenings and evenings become midnight scared of a revolution or an uproar hoping fire will not settle in the event. Some are upset, but truth is powerful. It makes the real President take office. It makes the real General take charge of an army with the purpose to push back the oppressions. That causes a major problem for what has come before and results in not to have people in a direction, not finding anything but madness, violence, and darkness.

The purpose would be to reform what was once displayed as principles that came with the nature religions. These parts that have been practiced before they were heard of and spread across the countries with documents in the tombs. Was the future foretold? Possibly. More of the brain was being used compared to the modern times. We are more pro anything sounds different made up teaching. It seems like revealing any part of the truth can turn into the category of a threat.

Now truth can come in different languages, dialects, ways of life, and symbols from hieroglyphics to English. So revealing truth can be forever because so much has been covered up for years. Many lies were told and still upheld because it sells. Still, we must let the truth be told.

We say what is that truth? People speak of what people listen to. It starts with history that has been written since the beginning of time. It starts with history that has been hidden. The history that has been rewritten with false teachings and words that form a different language. It starts with history that makes people mad because of the racism that has been expressed for centuries and they try to figure out why it has been allowed.

Why have people been taken out of books? Why has history been taken out of the Bible? Why has Christopher Columbus' name changed from birth and be allowed to steal and claim he discovered a land that was already occupied by the Indians. Why was it taught in history class and celebrated each year as Thanksgiving? Jesus' birthday is celebrated in December as Christmas, but he was born in the spring. Why is history a copy of Osiris and the mother of Isis?

Why do we have to pay for additional history that has to deal with our past history in which should be taught and known without money? Why were certain wars fought just for power? Why do Christians and Catholics war with the Illuminati because of the truth that overrides what they want to teach; not what was already said.

Why are we not showing the way for the troubled youth? Why are we not guiding them through troublesome times? Why are we not counseling to help with divorced couples and the youth who pay the most for the separation? Why are there no more recreational programs for the youth? Why is the government money spent on things that do not deal with helping our youth's education? Even Michael Jackson preached in his songs it starts with the kids if any change is to be done.

We have to teach the youth not to listen to anyone who does not have a message or is leading them down the wrong path. They must be taught to ask more questions if confused. They will not be looked at any different to how they are coming or represented.

Falling for ignorance is promising. Even though focusing is harder than it looks or feels, it is a must and part of the drive.

Some think of the money while others just think of their situation and they want and need to make it better. Worrying about if you make it to the end should not be in the equation. Who cares about the past? Who cares what mistakes you have made? Who cares about how many times you fall? All that matters is what you have learned for all what you have been through. What is important is your position now and what your goals are. Time never stops and it is of the essence.

We only lose time when we stop driving. Time will only stop when you stop focusing on your goals and your future plans. Elevation mentally and physically must always be done. Revelations are always being said. Once quitting becomes a vocabulary of the mind you stop fighting. You stop striving for richness. The rough path becomes greater and anxiety and stress fall upon the brain. Our words, voice, and actions have to be heard and felt across the nation and sought in other nations. Words have to always be inspiring and motivating so others can keep life and enjoyment alive. Remember there is always someone watching. There is always someone with new technology.

Mentally you have to be on point at all times for the sake of your path. Your physical has to be up to par. We must stay in shape and exercise for the physical health. We must live forever and words must be a part of the legacy that has been laid and preached for years and marched across the nation. Help is always needed and wanted. When you get the calling, listen to it and follow that calling. Follow that voice you hear. Follow that inspiration. If the path you have been looking for is sought to follow it. It's that prayer someone has been asking. It's that love someone has been yearning for. We all need that drive. That's when past professors can help us with that history or path. They can help us with the interpretation of a lesson.

We have Mother's Day. We also have Father's Day as well as Valentine's Day. Many days we celebrate to acknowledge those who helped and played their part in someone's life. Barbecues, weddings, parties, they all acknowledge the loved one has for another and giving recognition for the support one gives to another.

Chapter 25
Support Helps.

We all need it. Businesses, parades, baby showers, weddings, and relationships all need advice from somebody. Even financial help is needed and if it is given, ideas always arise. We all fall short and some get discouraged and stop trying. Ambition tends to fade. Drives lose power sometimes. Dreams sometimes get lost and begin to give ourselves and others excuses. Black becomes one's color like it rains every day.

It seems like you are under a cloud of judgment or darkness. You cannot allow yourself to fall in stages of misery. We get lost being unhappy. We lose sight being sad. Thinking hope cannot be seen and words become speechless. Courage plays a major part in life and the ability to overcome, not obstacles, but death in families. We must overcome things that have been inherited and maintained because of its structure.

Talking about others in a negative fashion comes with life because people are ignorant to their own self-centeredness. Speaking to face-to-face and explaining to them that you see a false play or foul ball can help one's growth.

Denial may come into effect because of guilt or ignorance. So we tell them the truth in a playful manner expecting the blind to catch it. Some do and some don't. The one that does changes slowly or catches the things they do. Why? They didn't see the truth at first, even with mirror images. The ones that don't will always be blind to the stages of elevation thinking the way they think or have been thinking is the true way. It has been working for them for a long time only to find out it has been the wrong way the entire time.

I had a short conversation with an older guy about why he was upset. He told me that another man asked him what high school he attends? The man got upset and said that it was none of his business. He asked what the reason for asking him that question. The man then attempted to explain to me that it was a very good reason why he did not see why he needed to know what high school he went to or even if he graduated at all. The real question was, had he furthered his education? He also wanted to know if he wanted to set up a program for the high school, in which the man had graduated from, to show the up and coming kids that education was important and they should graduate. If they dropped out, get their GED. He never really answered the question and was really offended by it. He did not have a high school diploma or a GED and that was the reason why he really got upset.

I understand that people may not like their outcome in life or the path they took, but why not want to educate those who are coming up in this society that we live in? Why not help them accomplish their goals? Regardless of age and character, it should not be a burden or crutch to where they should not further their dreams in becoming successful. There are many people of a younger age who do not know how to read or write with the proper vocabulary or spelling in which may discourage them from furthering their own education or life goals. Why not help them in their struggle and try to accomplish what they want to become. Why not help them with comprehension skills that are not carried far because of their inner problems.

One day I was watching an episode and I couldn't hear so I put on the closed caption so I could read it. I could tell the one who got upset because he could not read it. They started hissing and asking what was going on in the movie. Others walked away and started doing other things that would excite them at the time to substitute the fact that they could not read. It bothered me that they did not even make an attempt to ask questions but instead did other things hoping nobody noticed. Some did not notice and the day went on like it didn't even occur that people did not know how to read.

People are never really affected by their flaws until the flaws are put to a challenge or the obstacle puts them in a position where an attempt is made to make some kind of change to move forward toward positive steps. I guess this is why they have tutors to help those who have problems with a situation to help come up with a solution. Instead of being educated on guns and war strategies, the bullets of knowledge would travel through the mind of the youth in a positive way instead of a negative way.

We all in some shape, form or fashion know that education is the key to all problems. As I said before knowledge is beyond infinite. Education has to be learned by all people, from all levels…street dealers to restaurant workers to businessmen to politics. For years it has been emphasized how education is important. My question is, if education is so important, then why are schools having a hard time in the financial areas?

We as a nation are so worried about filling the rich pockets. We keep them settled either by stealing the money or some reason that it is used for more important things rather than what is needed. Who can we talk to about these issues and get some kind of solution along with good points? As it has been said, there's no award for helping. But a better future for our kids is priceless knowing that we control our own actions and thoughts and putting them into play is our own doing,

Never allow anyone to put a battery on your back and play on you like an Xbox. Know and understand that if you are on the top, all people will appear on your front step knocking on your door morning, afternoon, and evening. Then they will want to stay the night. When everything is all drunk, all is spent and the party is all over, you will see who stayed to clean up. Who will come over the next day knowing all the fun is over? No more drinks. No more money to be spent.

True friends are different from associates. Sometimes maybe clearer than others and blindness is a part of life but awareness has to be always on point. Sharpness. You must be up for all challenges. You may not catch or beat them all the time but you will be aware of them if approached twice.

Losing is a part of life, but you can control how many you lose if any. Flawless. Perfect. Immortal. Life is never really over. It just goes onto another life form. Living life according to nature is perfect.

Chapter 26
Nature's Religion.

It's a way of life; peace, harmony, and balance. We as humans lose focus but nature never does. It can only be disturbed in which its reaction is catastrophic. Once the lesson is learned depending on the action, it restores its natural habitat.

Peace. Beauty. Happiness. Freedom is better. No worries less problems. Stronger will power. Clearer thoughts. More sensible decisions. Always remember gray clouds are going to cover the sun, but as long as the sun rays shine through the clouds the days will always be promising. Besides the abuse, besides the oppression, besides the false words of discouragement from the haters and jealous people, we still shine.

Reflection from mirrors. Positive rays attract other positive insight and help. So keep searching. Keep pushing. Keep striving. Keep reaching because even though the sky's the limit there's more. There is more than what have discovered. There is more than what has been invested. There are more beautiful flowers to make the air feel natural and refreshing. There are more smiles to be seen and more thoughts to be given or taken in as helpful advice, so goals and destinations can be followed and pursued.

The world has so many beautiful places to be seen and so many mountains to touch and lakes and parts of the oceans to swim in. So many fish and so many animals to be seen. All parts of life. All with the very same gift that we all have and that's living free. Man interrupts harmony with a melody that is so cruel that causes confusion amongst people that have communication that leads a nation and culture. Our business seems like it is in others, wondering if they are doing better than they are, not really worried about their own situation and solutions, and the ways to overcome selfishness. We need to focus on how to change one's own self and inspire those who are both listening and lost. No more worries or problems with overcoming pride issues. No more 'we shall overcome'. No more drama. No more breaking peace deals and no more war on terrorism. What we consider terrorism is made from an action from the greed of power.

Once one knows about self, he/she can overcome their own sense of self-righteousness. Their future looks more promising and more adventurous. More powerful and rich. More dedicated and less effortless. More effective and less inappropriate. More mindful and less disrespect. Find the right music that you can vibe to. The music that goes with the sound that moves the heart with the beat that affects the soul. Find that love from the opposite sex that makes you review life with passion and patience. It makes you feel complete. It makes you feel whole with a companion that feels the same way towards you. It can be seen more or less heard. It can be heard in the words that one uses in a conversation. The look at life appears different. It appears less complicated. Less confusing. Goals seem more visible and less blurry. Love is nature's doing and man/woman's manifestation and understanding of its doing and feeling.

War disrupts the balance and causes havoc. Not only within you as a person but to a people as a group. It has been around since the people who were building to reach the heavens. In which I don't understand why God gave them different languages. It caused war amongst the people. The different languages caused different teachings and ways of life.

Who started the war? We will never know but only know how to play our part and let it not be chaos. Some let pride get in the way and egos are bigger with every audience playing on their characters and busting their self- esteem in a negative fashion. Some see other leaders and dislike them because they can't get the leader to follow them and come at them with a negative way attempting to shatter the glory or stop his smile from appearing on the faces of the happy. Negative energy cannot always be transformed into another and positive always weighs more but both of the two ways can be seen to the mirror and others. We think all we need is an army to feel big, but confidence can always be strong and it weighs a tremendous amount of weight.

Whenever you shine, shine bright enough so the blind can see you. Make a person want to be on your side because of the energy that is given off because of your aura or demeanor. The youth are always looking for those who can relate to them. They listen to what you actually have to say. Just make it modern instead of old ways. Even though the old ways are sometimes the better ways and sometimes it is too old but makes it sound good and look beautiful even to the ugly. Some just want someone to be there for them. Some just want a leader to follow. Some just want to hear that message to motivate them to create a new idea or encourage those to push harder.

Chapter 27
Accomplishing Goals.

Achieve more. Strive to reach the top of the ladder. Once you reached the top never forget how you started and never forget what it took to get there. You have to take care of yourself before you can take care of anybody else. Your intentions may be good but if you are not secure within yourself, it would not be fully accomplished because all of your strength is not into it. When you do something or help someone with a problem, put your all into it. Make a person say you are awesome. Why? You took a person's situation and made it your own and took the time out to solve it.

Tomorrow is never promised and that's why you live a day like it's your last. Never express anger towards another that makes an attempt to push your buttons. Yes it is easily said than done, and sometimes you may come out of character attempting to ignore it, but trying is better than dying.

Being tired of old things is the start of a new beginning. Closing doors behind you help maintain speed for the future you have mapped out by goals. Not allowing anyone in your way of your goals help you witness your own strength and ambition. Keeping past speeches, lectures, and movements alive can help your motivation to become advanced. Staying open-minded can help you see and understand things that were once misunderstood and could not see because of lack of knowledge. Keeping your mind fueled up with the positive energy as 'the little train that could' helps push harder when times get rough. Writing down goals can help keep you focused on achievements. Worrying about one's own self can and will help you continue being strong for life's obstacles.

Having support and not burning bridges will help you when needing that word or inspiration to achieve anything. Always think of others who give you support when and if goals are made. Never forget those who did not give when needed and use it as motivation to accomplish more.

Read as much as you can to get more insight of what is needed to study one's, class. Walking away from battles is not losing but making the smarter decision and winning the war by not fighting. You can always win by using the mind instead of using physical energy. I know being physical can sometimes win and make money as far as boxing but being physical does not win every battle. Thinking everything through thoroughly can and will help you with anything that requires decision making. Yes, we go through our own rough times.

Ups and downs. Speaking about it to a person you confide in will help you clear your plate which may be full of disappointments or challenges. As we live every day we learn different ways of approaching obstacles and handling them without doing too much. Life has its own ways of approaching you, but with the proper knowledge of knowing thyself helps deal with whatever comes at you.

Hard or soft. Fast or slow. Having the knowledge of what you are dealing with helps handle it a little better trying not to upset its ways of movement. It's rhythm. It's vibration. It's cycle as well as it's gender can help you understand it better rather than not knowing hurts you more than knowing what you are facing.

Meditation is helpful as well as breathing techniques. Understanding different principles and applying to your foundation helps figure out and solve issues that seem hard. It's better when you have support from loved ones or just from those who believe in you or your cause being persistent about your doings or in a workplace shows strength in your dedication in accomplishing something that you start. It shows loud and far. It can be seen on banners, Internet, or be talked about in social rooms or business conversations.

You want to be successful in all that you do. Failing is a part of life and only a learning lesson in how to grow. You would be surprised in how to grow. You would be surprised how many people you influence in a positive and negative way. People sometimes study others to learn their movements. To see what their outcome in any matter turns out to be. What obstacles they had to go through to win the battle either with a problem or just the battle between good and evil.

Do they take the same routine or make a new routine as one did. Other people's stories are learning lessons; life experiences in how things affect them emotionally. Sometimes people talk about it. Sometimes people don't speak about it. Sometimes people think they don't talk about it because they think they have something to hide. That is not always the matter.

Some go through so much physical and emotional pain, where speaking about it makes them remember something they tried hard to forget. They may hold it in and say there is no one to talk to and they are in their own rainstorm with no umbrella and no shelter from the cold. Some just would like to cry out but cash out in all the wrong places because they hurt. Not intentionally to hurt another, but pain runs deep. Some just shell up and never speak a complete sentence again. Some who don't understand may say that a person is weird because they don't speak then start to clown them because their style is different. It only makes things worst. It only complicates things more. It only makes things worse than what is called for. You may feel the wind stop blowing. The air gets dry and the battle begins to be lost because of no help. No understanding and no hope.

It begins to fade to black and the color of light is now a shadow. The ignorant of others because of selfishness, becomes a problem to you and the little things that you once let pass now bothers you. Things get irritated and trouble begins to grow. Why? All because of misunderstandings. Some just want to stay in the closet so no more hurt can be applied, but don't because they don't want to show others how upset they are.

To give the response, it's nothing you could do about it. The fact of being alone weighs a lot. Sleep starts to come sooner and longer than normal. Some began to take anxiety pills. Some start talking to them self. Some start to lose one's mind because they feel like there is no one to talk to. They only give advice and not really help them financially as needed.

No one will see your social connection is closing and that window of opportunity is gone. Doors are shut and locked no more are let in. Doors are shut and locked and none will be let in. Not because of what you did but what you are going through. No one wants to take on a problem that's not theirs. But they will watch you go to crap and talk about you because the situation you are in. It may not even be your fault but because no questions are asked some come up with their own assumptions and others will entertain it because of gossip.

Gossip. Some people do not like their business in other people's mouths, and would rather keep to themselves but evil plays a part in life. You need a bad guy. You need someone to take the blame. Someone to take the blame…someone to point the finger and to say they did it.

No glory. In the dark. Only the cold discomfort. There is no sunshine when the cold sets in. No rainbow when your eyes are not set on goals and ways to improve yourself. Ways to better. Ways to navigate in or out of obstacles. There's always room for improvement within one's self. There's always another mountain not seen. Do not let the height of the mountain discourage you from climbing over it. Don't let it discourage you and turn you around.

Rethink your position. Do not allow your mind to say I can't do it. With knowing every day is something new and different, you have to be aware and wise enough to know how to walk that line. If you don't there is always somebody willing to help someone who has been through that same situation and now has the knowledge to shed light upon the blind.

Nothing is actually hard and all situations can be resolved. If anything can be done, no matter what position you are in anything is possible. If heaven can disappear and reappear without anybody knowing how can you get things done in the midst of a hurricane? All it takes is patience and the knowledge. Research and study all can be learned and taught. Everybody speaks of change, but are you willing to change the way you think to prove to yourself that life is different and possibly better outside your current environment.

Say to yourself, "This day is different and what happened yesterday may not happen today. What will occur today foretells what happens tomorrow."

To gather information is always helpful for the future and not taking it at face value. Examining the words that are being used will help one understand the nature of its element and its power that it possess. What goals are one's powers if you can use or not? You are given the power to fight only life's problems from foes that are against your movements; that is against your will, and that is against your cause. Those that want to see you fail and not let you progress and be known to those who wait and seek general knowledge and assistance to overcome a situation that they might not know anything about.

You have those who have other intentions with hidden causes. They infiltrate the line you are stomping on. Interrupt the music by thumping to another tune. You cannot allow yourself to be broken or shattered because times get hard or you feel like you don't have any assistance with your matter. As I said, we do get false hope. We do get false teachings. We do get false dreams.

Dreams that get sold in the wind of prayer. We are lied to by those who take advantage of a situation and get the insight to get rid of its lessons of history so it would not continue to be practiced because they want their own lessons to be recognized and taught as truth but wrong.

They say you get the money and after that power; then after the power, you get the respect. Its funny money changes a person's aspect on life. It alters who you are and adds to the loss sight of the value of one's culture. The value of life is priceless, but one of the powers of money is greed to the devil and hatred towards others. Focusing is no longer an issue because money handles all that is in need.

Once you have that power to do as you please, overcome what? Judge who? Walk what line? If not careful and handled wisely, evilness takes over with corruption and leaders are hushed in a way that can't be seen. Even medical cures are added to the black market trade. The more you have the more power you have. Respect comes from what you do with money and power. Some get respect first then get the power.

No fear…Just encouragements. Power becomes a struggle because of those who don't have it. Power becomes a struggle for those who are in a fit of rage because their light is not shining as bright; because their journey has no room for power. What you seek is what you get. It's about honor and loyalty.

Chapter 28
Courage And Valor.
A Soldier's Loyalty.

Time is everything. If used properly all that is needed to be done could be done and more time is at hand. It all depends on what a person wants. What you seek. What you cherish. They say 'a man's trash is another woman treasure'. We sometimes don't know what we have or we do not appreciate it until another person has it and sees the value and cherishes it with everything they have.

Nothing is done quickly expecting results right away. That's when that patience thing kicks in. It feels good to be on top and a shame to be at the bottom. It also feels good to be king or queen. As long as you have your listeners, your followers, your disciples, your teachings, and studies can always be heard just like speeches are still being taught until today from years plus ago.

If you don't know what you are looking for, how would you know if it is in front of your face or not? A lot of things come from tunes. If your heart is scorn, it may be hard to intake a person's interest. You may miss many opportunities because of hurt and another person's pride, ego or just jealousy and even greed.

'Keep your head up' is the only statement that stays in the mind when something happens wrong or out of place. When a person is incarcerated it hurts or just losing someone that you may love due to life. No one can tell when a person will pass. Peace is the main aspect because you get to enjoy the memories and presence of that person. Some tattooed names and pictures are always being taken. Love runs deep and everybody experiences it in all fashions; in everything and in everybody; people, places, and things.

Improving yourself in life comes with change with the century's evolution. Things become easier but on another aspect, things become harder because of technology. It makes things easy to see and use automatically, and manually things are forgotten and lost.

Racism and Prejudice. Even when you think things have calmed down in America the past actions of racism and prejudice still finds its way of resurfacing in the faces of some. The way parents were taught and they continue to teach their children the same lessons expressed the same way today. It's no longer so much of black on black crimes or race on race crimes that affect the nation. It's race on different race crimes.

Authorities have the weapon and have the authority to shoot if they feel their life has been threatened. Instead of using it in a proper manner, they use it to justify their unlawful actions. It is as though they signed an oath. It is a requirement to get backup for all officers in law. Improper behavior, persuasive force, false reports, the list goes on and on, and most get swept under the rug.

If an uproar happens, they will do anything to stop it but deal with the actual person in involved in accordingly the way they aren't which is unjustified. We as a nation have supposedly one leader and he is considered the president along with others who control things in the background. They can't take care of everything but try to address many issues at hand near and far.

The problem that is continuously expressed because of negligent from our government is getting bigger and nothing really gets done until it hits their own backyard. That's when the situation has to be handled, but before that happens, no one cares. This is not a life lesson. This is not what they teach us in school. They do not tell you how to handle situations that involve racism. It alive every day in most homes depending on what has been taught in the home. It depends on what they experience with their life journey in dealing with other people.

Life is not fun to deal with because of the obstacles that come with it. Experience teaches you how to deal with things that come your way again depending on the path you take. People are harsh and cruel and life can be learned in a harsh way. One person affected by harsh ways reacts in a way that could cause bodily harm to others. Those who stand on the outside looking in, only judge you but do not know what you have been through or taught by such acclaimed teacher.

People are harmed by others through shooting in schools or shooting of innocent people who are not armed and should not be affected by another person's madness. They are because the person claims self-defense or pleads the insanity role. When cleaning a house all dust and vents have to be cleaned up and out. Everything has to be whipped down and double checked because dust can linger everywhere. Why? To keep things going in an orderly fashion and to make sure the wrong will not be caught because of mistakes they have made to bring down organizations that are built on corruption. As I said God does not like ugly but not too fond of pretty.

Instead of helping others by telling the truth people will lie because they may see others looking or doing better than them. Some see it and some are blind to its facts. When presented with the truth to be heard, their ears are so clogged, where if getting cleaned, people still wouldn't want that lesson.

Why? Again because people don't want to hear things that are new. It changes their mind about the way they have been looking at the truth. What they once knew to be right is wrong. Rerouting and learning something new is hard. People are set in ways that get them by what was working until thrown off the tracks going the same direction but moving differently. Sometimes once they are in, they find the new ways better than the old.

There is nothing wrong with new, and fear should not be in the mind of those who want and need change. Each generation is different from the last. Time may get easier and better because of what the previous generation did. They paved the way. They made it harder for the knowledge to be taught because they didn't take the time out to learn it. People may look and take the easy road out. Thinking it's a better way to shorten what needs to be done, but it only shortened the understanding and full knowledge of what has to be done and learned.

The question that matters is, what is the truth? If we are presented with the truth what will we do with it? Better yet, will we notice it or get tied down our old ways and we will not acknowledge it.

Truth is in history. Truth is hidden. Truth is a combination of elements, principles, and teachings that can be traced back to the beginning of time; things that can be researched and studied; things that have always been planted in the roots of the formation of society. Truth is buried in tombs, fallen temples, or in vaults that are guarded so all will not see. Truth has always been told but not all listen because of the media and the government that tries to makes more sense out of things than the truth, but does it?

We accept it because we don't have the research or go look for it. With the technology that we live with today, you should never get tired of looking for the truth. If anything, you should never stop searching. For the answer you are looking for is out there.

Somebody has said the answer to your problem is possibly written it down, just titled a little differently. We have to stay in the race because this marvelous race travels around the world. The race starts with a goal and comes wit a pace. If an idea is not thought of, you will not know the race called, "Life". Yes, I said, "Life". Life is short but the faster you learn what you are racing for and against, life becomes easier and with less stress.

With less stress, ambition grows bigger and hunger becomes an everyday thing; hungry for more...thirsty for knowledge. Music never stops. It keeps playing every minute, every day; every part of the nation. Some are hard tunes and some are soft, but music is 'the cure to the soul' as I say. Now all around the world, there is a different tune, but people suffer from the same problems; such as famine, diseases, lack of love for each other, all in the rim of ruining the earth's atmosphere. We have hunger issues all around the world.

We as a nation are so worried about who has bigger weapons. Who has the most power and so on and so on? The earth itself can produce more than enough food for everyone. If our food supply was managed properly along with the communication from other nations, we could stop the ratio of who does not get enough to each other. When the magnitude of 7.0 earthquakes struck Haiti that killed more than 300,000 people and an additional number in the millions of homeless; we not only as a nation but the world as a whole should have been there to show support.

All nations are not enriched like the United States but with the combined help, we could have made a huge difference instead of worrying about the economy. How can any nation come out of tranquility if everybody worries about power instead of the life God has given all? We have diseases all over, such as diarrhea, HIV/ AIDS, malaria, and many other life-threatening diseases that destroy mankind. We still do not have the cure for the Ebola virus but when a cure is developed in the rain forest, it's still some out there.

As the population grows theses diseases spread with nothing to stop them. It's all about the all mighty dollar to prevent you from suffering a lot. They say if people care so much, donate to societies that have foundations to find and help cure those who have those diseases. Polluting the earth does not help much either. We pollute the earth at a tremendous degree. It does not look like we care at all and yet preach about global warming, low water levels, toxic water, and much more. We as human beings have the obligation to reverse those acts but are so tied up with everyday life we don't have time to support groups. These groups are doing some things like raising awareness of environmental issues to educate those who are paying attention to the atmosphere around them; big truck smoke, fires, hair sprays, oil spills, the list go on and on.

But what does one do when presented with the truth? What are we as individuals doing to help or destroy the earth that we get natural resources from and praise so gladly? You have people like Al Gore who has ties in the political field that televised these very same issues that I am presenting but there have not been many people who took heed. People who rather look at reality television which is not really reality at all or stay tuned to the Internet but not to research the things that are being said.

People say as long as it does not hit home what's the reason to worry about it? People entertain things that are not major issues and really affect any person as a whole. You have people out there whose purpose is to help you succeed in life or whatever the problems are in which you are going through.

Many people listen to the radio now more than before. Some radio stations allow educational speeches on their stations knowing those who do listen will continue to listen and advise others to tune in. They hope expressing thoughts about global issues will help others express how others feel and more support may rise. We always have to feel confident that things we do to solve a problem will work because not trying to find a solution to the problem creates more problems. Nobody will give. People who show support are the ones who want to see you survive or succeed.

Some leaders are born leaders. Some just have to realize what they have. That starts within one's self. Some go through some type of tragedy to realize it and some go through a depression to see true talent. Some realize it early and some realize it late but once you realize it, they teach others who are younger.

"Believe half of what you see and less than what you hear." Lies are always being told and shown. You don't have to go to school to be a leader. It starts within you. Once on the path to success, you may feel as though you want to give back you to your community or to the school or company that helped you. Know this in life, every good deed will not be recognized or acknowledged by all or even the ones you would like to acknowledge the good you do. You may do good things, send to others because you want to do them out of the kindness of your heart and really don't care of the acknowledgment or not as long as the ones you are doing it forgets it, you are happy.

Always remember this as well, if you do one innocent thing, it's going to be heard across the world. People may look at you messed up, praying for your downfall. You are a menace to society if committed a crime. Everything you have done well is no longer good. You are bad. Society eats up things like that. If you fail it gives them time to step on you and prove the lies that have been ever told to be right. It just looks that way.

Chapter 29
"Crabs In A Barrel."

People figure, if you make it, it makes them look ugly to others. You don't need to prove anything to anybody but yourself. That's the only one that loves you unconditionally. The only one that will keep you sane. The only one that will pick you up when you fall hard or soft. You must understand there are cruel people in the world. Some think they know it all and some that want their lies to be the truth. It's the inner demon within you, by any means to succeed. Know and understand this, some people do illegal things to get themselves out of their situation, to make things better. To make things easier because all positive they were doing did not make it in and out. Some get caught up in the mix and don't want to leave and some get caught trying to get that little pay to pay that outstanding bill or car note, or tuition.

Now that a person is caught, they look like the worst person in the world. Every good thing is nonexistence. You are the world's worst nightmare. In the end, you are the one who has to live with your decision. You are the only one who has to still stand your ground against judgmental people. Whatever your decision was or is, make it the best. While doing right or wrong, think of others in the midst of doing you. Never cross a person just to attempt to succeed.

Two step like a dance. Line dance like it's your last, knowing this journey in life is not over until one is in the grave. It still goes on and lives by your followers, your children, or the one you have left the torch to. Succeed with every passion. Grow in life in the prospect of riches of knowledge and wisdom that could be spread to others to learn and teach how to be successful and to reach their ultimate goals.

Whatever the goal is; do it to the best of your ability. Do it like it's your last time. Do it not tomorrow, but knowing when the end comes it starts a new beginning. You can look back at your accomplishments and be proud of yourself because at one time you may have said, it can't be done. It's too hard. I have no help. All types of excuses that tend to destroy you. No one says anything in life is easy. Nothing in life is free and anything you want you have to work hard to get it and if given to you by blessing you must work harder to maintain it.

With Life comes big responsibilities; some fail and some succeed. If failed, you can only blame yourself for not going harder and if you succeed, you can thank yourself and those who showed you support and believed that you could.

Your reason for justice…your freedom of speech. As you journey to freedom, the land is furthered with help. Never forget there are people who are jealous, as well as, the other five devils who may pray on your downfall. Who may not want to see you succeed because they have failed in this game of life, this board game of chess. Life has its own way of working out. Confusion can fool anybody, even the smartest man or woman. Just like it takes a lot to raise a child, it takes a lot to succeed in life.

Doors may not be open when you want. Windows may be closed. Nobody picking up the phone. Can't get a loan because you may not have collateral. All kinds of loopholes come with succeeding in life. Always keep in mind that you can do it. There are so many people who went from rags to riches without inheritance.

Never waste time partnering with those who are not concerned in succeeding in life. Never stop trying to succeed in your dreams because you want to join those so-called friends who you think are winning. Some days may be worst than others and some days may be more active than others. You may at times say to yourself you need a vacation. Once that thought appears in the mind, think about where you are trying to get to and where you came from to get there and keep on pushing. The changes you may have to take will come with losing those so-called friends, but it will pay off in the long run.

People will look at you differently because you have changed your ways have changed. Not because you have changed as a person, but because your ways of approaching life with a different swag as I call it; a different style. You may even get made fun of in a negative way saying you may have forgotten about them.

Remember always when at the bottom some may want you to stay at the bottom because it makes them feel like they are doing something right or because it may make them feel better. Your success may make them look bad. You may have to learn to avoid old crowds and surround yourself with people who are succeeding in life. Surround yourself with people who want more than just sitting around and doing nothing to get ahead or out of their current situation. Always remember there are some people who came from that same bottom you came from and sometimes don't understand what the bottom is because they were not raised in certain ways you have. Everybody's path is different depending on where you want to get to and can relate to one another in some shape, form, fashion, or size and all have the ultimate goal and that is to be successful.

Don't forget on the way to the top what was said to get from the bottom, from whom said it when you didn't have it when you were struggling to find a way out. Some may even come up with lies so people can believe them. Stay focused, and use those negative sayings as energy that will fuel your ambition; inspiration to live and motivation to do more.

Just a dream you may one day wake up from. Your labor that you paved the way. Music sounds different now and the air tastes refreshing. You will gain followers positively. Always appreciate what one does for you along your path and the cause they do things for. Love you or not but never be used. People may even try to succeed off your success. Some may even want to ride in the same car as you are in. Some may even praise your name only to gain something personal from it. Instead of asking, they manipulate. Instead of helping, they may try to make fun of you. Positive people love your drive, your passion, your ambition, and your power. You may even want to change your name for a new beginning, a fresh start.

That drive becomes more powerful. Move in a more militant way. Move more focused than before or when you started. Your stride is longer. Dreams start to appear with every move. Things that were once hard are a little easier. As sitting back you must look at all the hard work you have done and where it got you from. You may have been in the hole. You may have been in the closet.

Life is a double-edged sword holding it is not easy but all you have to do is close your mouth and listen more. Listen to all the signs and warnings. Illegal punches. Low blows. Watch all things and people knowing their intentions may not all be positive or in your favor. Watch all ditches and pot holes knowing they all cannot be avoided. Attempt not to repeat the same ways or move that are negative. Take a different way back home or where you came from. Smokescreen those who are aware of your path, that wants to join too because of your success. Dilute the water in which your haters drink. Ignore the words that may be heart-breaking.

Words that do not motivate you or help you in your path to success. Know in the end of your path you have chosen you will see what you have built all through elevation and destroying all which you have stood for. The foundation that has been laid down and the house that has been built high enough to reach the clouds. Not to be blown away but out of the reach of those who want to see you fail. Those who want to see you accomplish nothing that would allow you to move forward. Forget what you pray for. Forget how much support you may have. You have those who may plot against your wishes. Just keep your mind focused on your goals. Keep your hands clean from illegal substances and movements and clear from the blurred vision that may not allow you to see in front of you. Even when success is near, still push for more. Even if money is made and you may feel a little comfortable strive for more.

Feel free from trouble. Feel free from worries. Rain does not always bring a gloomy day. The air that blows with the winds of nature feels so refreshing that you breath taken inhaled and exhaled are deep. You may feel at that moment anything can be accomplished in which is true. Even when situations are tight and things become stressful. Let it rain on your face and look to the sky and let your thoughts of stress and expression be released into what we inhale as air and exhale what feeds the trees. The circle of life we say all bonds with each other and nature takes its course and rules the land in which we love. The earth will rotate and the stars will always glow electrons and keep you focused achievements. Worrying about one own self can and will help you continue being strong for life obstacles. Having support and not burning bridges will help you when needing that word or inspiration to achieve anything. Always think of others that give you support when and if goals are made, never forget those who did not give when needed and use it as motivation to accomplish more. Read as much as you can to get more insight of what is needed to study one's class. Walking away from battles is not losing but making the smarter decision and winning the war by not fighting. You can always win by using the mind instead of using the physical. I know using the physical can sometimes win and make money as far as a boxing but cannot win every battle. Thinking everything through thoroughly can and will help you with anything that requires decision making. Yes, we go through our own rough times.

Ups and downs. Speaking about it to a person you confined in will help you clear your plate that may be full of disappointments or challenges. As we live every day we learn different ways of approaching obstacles and handling them without doing too much. Life has its own ways of approaching you, but with the proper knowledge of knowing thyself helps deal with whatever comes at you.

Hard or soft. Fast or slow. Having the knowledge of what you are dealing with helps handle it a little better trying not to upset its ways of movement. It's rhythm. It's vibration. It's cycle as well as it's gender can help you understand it better rather than not knowing hurts you more than knowing what you are facing self-medication is helpful, as well as, breathing techniques. Understanding different principles and applying to your foundation helps figure out and solve issues that seem hard. It's better when you have support from loved ones or just from those who believe in you, or your cause being persistent about your doings, or in a workplace shows strength in your dedication in accomplishing something that you start.

It shows loud and far. It can be seen on banners, internet, or/and being talked about in social rooms or business conversations. You want to be successful in all what you do but failing is a part of life but only a learning lesson in how to grow. You would be surprised in how to grow. You would be surprised how many people you influence in a positive and negative way. People sometimes study others to learn their movements. To see what their outcome in any matter turns out to be. What obstacles they had to go through to win the battle either with a problem or just the battle between good and evil.

Do they take the same routine or make as one did. Other people's stories are learning lessons. Their life experiences and how things affect them emotionally. Sometimes people talk about it just because they think if you don't speak about it, you have something to hide. That is not always the case. Some go through so much physical and emotional pain, whereas through speaking about it makes them remember something they try hard to forget.

They may hold it in and say there is no one to talk to, and they are on their own with no umbrella from the rain, and no shelter from the cold. Some just would like to cry out, but cash out in all the wrong places because they hurt. Not intentionally to hurt another, but pain runs deep.

Some just shell up, and never speak a complete sentence again. Some who don't understand may say that a person is weird because they don't speak then start to clown them because their style is different. It only makes things worst. It only complicates things more. It only makes things worst than what is called for.

You may feel the wind stop blowing. The air gets dry and the battle begins to be lost because of no help. No understanding and no hope. It begins to fade to black and the color of light is now a shadow. The ignorant of others because of selfishness becomes a problem to you and the little things that you once let pass now bothers you. Things get irritated and trouble begins to grow. Why? All because of misunderstandings.

Some just want to stay in the closet so no more hurt can be applied but don't because they don't want to show others how upset they are. To give the response, it's nothing you could do about it. The fact of being alone weighs a lot. Sleep starts to come sooner and longer than normal Some began to take anxiety pills.

Start talking to them self. Start to lose one's mind because they feel like they can only give like there is no one to talk to because they can only give advice and not really help them financially as needed. No one will see your social connection is closing and that window of opportunity is gone.

Doors are shut and locked no more be let in. Doors are shut and locked and no one will let you in. Not because of what did, but what you are going through. No wants to take on a problem that's not theirs, but they watch you go to crap, and they will watch you go to crap, and talk about you because the situation you are in. It may not even be your fault, but because no questions are asked some come up with their own assumptions and others will entertain it because of gossip. Some people do not like their business in other people's mouths and would rather keep to themselves but evil plays a part in life. You need a bad guy. Someone to take the blame. Someone to point the finger and to say they did it. No glory in the dark.

Only the cold discomfort. There is no sunshine when the cold sets in. No rainbow when your eyes are not set on goals and ways to improve yourself. Ways to better. Ways to navigate in or out of obstacles. There is always room for improvement within one's self. There is always another mountain that has not been seen. Do not let how high the mountain is discouraging you from climbing over it. Don't let it discourage you and turn around.

To rethink your position. To allow your mind to say I can't do it. With knowing every day is something new and different, you have to be aware and wise enough to know how to walk that line and if you don't there is always somebody willing to help, someone who has been through that same situation and now has the knowledge to shed light upon the blind.

Nothing is actually hard and all situations can be resolved. If anything can be done, no matter what position you are in, anything is possible. If heaven can disappear and reappear without anybody knowing. How can you get things done in the midst of a hurricane? All it takes is patience and the knowledge. Research and study all can be learned and taught.

Everybody speaks of change, but are you willing to change the way you think to prove to yourself that life is different, and possibly better outside your current environment. Saying to yourself, "This day is different. And what happened yesterday, may not happen today and what will occur today will foretell what happens tomorrow." To gather information is always helpful for the future and not taking it at face value. Examining the words that are being used will help one understand the nature of its element and its power that it possess.

What goals are one's power if you can use or not. You are given the power to fight only life's problems but from those that are against your movements. From those that are against your will. From those that are against your cause. Those that want to see you fail and not let your progress be known to those who wait and seek general knowledge and assistance to overcome. A situation that they might not know anything about. You have those who have other intentions with hidden causes. They infiltrate the line you are stomping on. Interrupt the music by thumping to another tune. You cannot allow yourself to break or shatter because times get hard or you feel like you don't have any assistance with your matter. As I said we do get false hope.

We do get false teachings. Dreams that get sold in the wind of prayer. Those who take advantage of a situation and get the insight to get rid of its lessons of history so it would not continue to be practiced because they want their own lessons to be recognized and taught as truth but wrong. They say you get the money and after the power then after the power, you get the respect. Its funny money changes a person's perspective on life. It alters who you are and loses sight of the value of culture.

The value of life is priceless but the power of love for money is greed to the devil and hatred towards others. Focusing is no longer an issue because money handles all that is in need. Now that you have that power to do as you please, to overcome what? Judge who? Walk what line?

Evil takes over with corruption and leaders are hushed in a way that can't be seen. Even medical cures become part of the black market trade. The more you have the more power you have. Respect comes from what you do with money and power. Some get respect first, then comes the power.

No fear. Just encouragements. Power becomes a struggle because of those who don't have it. Those who are in a fit of rage because their light is not shining as bright. Because their journey has no room for power. What you seek is what you get. It's about honor and loyalty. Courage and valor. A soldiers loyalty. Time is everything. If used properly all that is needed to be done could be done and more time is at hand, all depending what a person wants. What you seek. What you cherish.

They say what a man's trash is another woman's treasure. We sometimes don't know what we have or not appreciate until another person has it and sees the value and cherishes it with everything they have.

Nothing should be done quickly expecting results right away. That's when that patience thing kicks in. It feels good to be on top and a shame to be at the bottom. It also feels good to be king or queen. As long as you have your listeners, your followers, your disciples, your teachings, and studies can always be heard; just like speeches are still being taught today from years plus ago.

If we don't know what we are looking for, how would we know if it is in front of our face or not? A lot of things come from tunes. If your heart is scorn, it may be hard to take in a person's interest. You may miss many opportunities because of hurt and another person's pride.

Ego or just jealousy and even greed. "Keep your head up" is the only statement that stays in the mind when something happens wrong or out of place. When a person is incarcerated it hurts or just losing someone that you may love due to life. No one can tell when a person will pass. Peace is the main aspect because you get to enjoy the memories and presence of that person. Some tattooed names and picture are always being taken. Love runs deep and everybody experiences it in all fashions.

In everything and in everybody, people, places, and things, improving yourself in life comes with change with the century's evolution. Things become easier but on other aspect, things become harder because of technology. It makes things easy to see and use automatically and manually. Things are forgotten and lost. Even when you think things have calmed down in America the past actions of racism and prejudice still finds its way resurfacing in the faces of some.

The way parents were taught has taught their children the same lessons in which they have been and are still being expressed today. It's no longer so much of black on black crime or race on race crime that affect the nation. It's race on different race crimes. The authority has the weapon to shoot if they feel their life has been threatened. Instead of using authority in a proper manner, they use it to justify their unlawful actions. They signed an oath that it is a requirement to have a backup of all officers in the law.

Improper behavior, persuasive force, false reports, the list goes on and on and most get swept under the rug. If there is an uproar they will do anything to stop it and will not deal with the actual person in which is involved in accordantly the way they ant which is unjustified.

We as a nation supposedly have one leader and he is considered the President. Along with others, the President and they control things in the background. They can't take care of everything but try to address many issues at hand near and far. The problem that continuously is expressed because of negligence from our government is getting bigger and nothing really gets done until it hits their own backyard. That's when the situation has to be handled, but before that happens, no one cares.

This is not a life lesson. This is not what they teach you in school. They do not tell you how to handle situations that involve racism. It lives every day in most homes depending on what has been taught in the home and what they experience with their life journey in dealing with other people. Life is not fun to deal with because of the obstacles that come with it.

Life teaches us how to deal with things that come our way, again and again, depending on the path you take. People are harsh and cruel. Life can be learned in a harsh way. A person that is affected by these ways reacts in a way that could cause bodily harm to others. Those who stand on the outside looking in not only judge you but do not know what you have been through or taught by such an acclaimed teacher (life).

Shooting in schools or shooting of innocent people, who are not armed and should not be affected by another person's madness, but yet some claim self-defense or plead the insanity role. When cleaning a house all dust and vents have to be cleaned up and out. Everything has to be whipped down and double checked because dust can linger everywhere. Why? To keep things going in an orderly fashion and to make sure wrong will not be caught.

Mistakes made to bring down organizations are built on corruption. As I said God does not like ugly but not too fond of pretty. Instead of helping others by telling the truth people will lie. They may see others looking or doing better than them. Some see it and some are blind to its facts and when presented with the truth, their ears are so clogged. If even if they were cleaned people still wouldn't want that lesson. Why? Again because people don't want to hear things that are new. It changes their motives about how they have been looking at the truth. What they once knew to be right is wrong; rerouting and learning something new is hard. You are set in ways that get you by and it was working, until now you're thrown off the tracks going the same direction but moving differently. Sometimes new ways are better than the old.

There is nothing wrong with new. Fear should not be in the mind of those who want and need change. Each generation is different from the last. Time may get easier and better because of what the previous generation did. They pave the way. They make it harder for the knowledge to be taught because they didn't take the time out to learn it. People may look and take the easy road out. Thinking it's a better way to shorten what needs to be done but it only shortens the understanding and full knowledge of what has to be done and learned.

Chapter 30
Hungry for More.
Thirsty for knowledge.

Music never stops. It keeps playing every minute every day and in every part of the nation. Some are hard tunes and some are soft but music is the cure to the soul as I say. Now all around the world, life plays a different tune, we all suffer from the same problems such as famine, diseases, lack of love for each other, all in the rim of ruining the earth's atmosphere.

We have hunger issues all around the world. We as a nation are so worried about who has bigger weapons? Who has the most power and so on and so on? The earth itself can produce more than enough food for everyone.

If our food supply was managed properly along with the communication from other nations, we could stop the ratio of who does not get enough. When the 7.0 magnitude earthquake struck Haiti and killed more than 300,000 people, and an additional number of the millions homeless. We not only as a nation but the world as a whole should have been there to show support. All nations are not as enriched like the United States but with the combined help, we could have made a huge difference instead of worrying about the economy. How can our nation be so tranquil if everybody is worried about power instead of the life God has given all?

We have diseases all over such as diarrhea, HIV/ AIDS, malaria, and much other life-threatening diseases that destroy mankind. We still do not have the cure for the Ebola virus but even when a cure is developed in the rain forest it will still remain out there.

As the population grows these diseases spread with nothing to stop it. It's all about the all mighty dollar. I could prevent us from suffering a lot. They say if people care so much, donate to societies that have foundations to find and help cure those who have those diseases and polluting the earth does not help much either. We pollute the earth at a tremendous degree in which it does not look like we care at all but yet preach about global warming, low water levels, toxic water, and much more.

We as human beings have the obligation to reverse those acts but are so tied up with everyday life. We don't have time to support groups that are doing things like raising awareness of environmental issues to educate those who are paying attention to the atmosphere around them. Big truck smoke, fires, hair sprays, oil spills, the list go on and on but what do one do when presented with the truth. What we as individuals are doing to help or destroy the earth that we get natural resources from and praise so gladly.

You have people like Al Gore who has ties in the political field that televised these very same issues that I am presenting but there have not been many people who took heed. People who rather look at reality television which is not really reality at all or stay tuned to the Internet but not research the things that are being said. People say as long as it does not hit home what's the reason to worry about it. People entertain things that are not issues and things that really do not affect anyone as a whole.

You have people out there where their purpose is to help others succeed in life. Or help with whatever problems you are going through. We all listen to the radio now more than before. Some radio stations allow educational speeches on their stations knowing those who do listen will continue to listen and advise others to tune in. They hope that expressing thoughts about global issues will help others express how others feel and more support may arise.

We always have to feel confident that things we do to solve a problem will work because not trying to find a solution to the problem creates more problems. Nobody will give and show support, as much as, the ones who want to see you survive or succeed.

Leaders are born leaders. Some just have to realize what they have. That starts within one's self. Some go through some type of tragedy to realize it and some go through a depression to see true talent. Some realize it early and some realize it late. But I suggest once you realize it, teach others who are younger than you.

"Believe half of what you see and less of what you hear." Lies are always being told and shown. You don't have to go to school to be a leader. It starts within you. Once on the path to success, you may feel as though you want to give back to your community or to the school, or to the company that helped you.

Know this, in life, every good deed will not be recognized or acknowledged by all or even the ones you would like to acknowledge the good you do.

You may do things well to others because you want to do them out of the kindness of your heart and you really don't care for the acknowledgment or not as long as the ones you are doing it forgets it, you are happy.

Always remember this as well, if you do one innocent thing, it's going to be heard across the world. People may look at you messed up. Praying for your downfall. You are a menace to society if you commit a crime. Every good thing you have done is no longer good. You are bad. Society eats at things like that. If you fail it gives them time to step on you and prove the lies that have always been told to be right. It just looks that way.

Crabs in a barrel. People figure, if you make it, it makes them look ugly to others. You don't need to prove anything to anybody but yourself. You're the only one that loves you unconditionally. The only one that will keep you sane. The only one that will pick you up when you fall hard or soft. You must understand there are cruel people in the world. Some think they know it all and some that want their lies to be the truth.

It's the inner demon within you. By any means to succeed. Know and understand this, some people do illegal things to get themselves out of their situation. To make things better. To make things easier because all the positive things they were doing did not quite make it in and out. Some get caught up in the mix and don't want to leave. Some get caught trying pay that outstanding bill or car note. A tuition.

Now that you are caught, you look like the worst person in the world. Every good thing is nonexistent. You are the world's worst nightmare. In the end, you are the one who has to live with your decision. You are the only one who has to still stand your ground against judgmental people. Whatever your decision was or is, make it for the best. While doing right or wrong, think of others in the midst of doing you. Never cross a person just to attempt to succeed. Two step like a dance. Line dance like it's your last knowing this journey in life is not over until you are in the grave.

Succeed with every passion for growing in life in the prospect of riches of knowledge and wisdom that could be spread to others to learn and teach how to be successful and to reach their ultimate goals. Whatever the goal is, do it to the best of your ability. Do it like it's your last time. Do it not tomorrow knowing when the end comes to start a new beginning. You can look back at your accomplishments and be proud of yourself because at one time you may have said, "it can't be done. It's too hard. I have no help."

All types of excuses that tend to destroy you. No one says anything in life is easy. Nothing in life is free and anything you want, you have to work hard to get it or it may be given to you by blessing. Sometimes you must work harder to maintain it. Life is a big responsibility . Some fail and some succeed. If you fail, you can only blame yourself for not going harder and if you succeed, you can thank yourself and those who showed you support and believed that you could.

Never forget there are people who are jealous and who may pray for your downfall. People who may not want to see you succeed because they have failed in this game of life. This board game of chess. Life has its own way of working out. Confusion can fool anybody, even the smartest man or woman. Just like it takes a lot to raise a child, it takes a lot to succeed in life.

Doors may not be open when you want. Windows may be closed. Nobody picks up the phone when you call. You can't get a loan because you may not have collateral. All kinds of loopholes come with succeeding in life. Always keep in mind that you can do it.

There are so many people who went from rags to riches without inheritance. Never waste time partnering with those who are not concerned in succeeding in life. Never stop trying to succeed in your dreams because you want to join those so-called friends who you think are winning. Some days may be worst than others and some days may be more active than others. You may at times say to yourself you need a vacation. Once that thought appears in the mind, think about where you are trying to get to and where you came from to get there and keep on pushing.

The changes you may have to take will come with losing those so-called friends, but it will pay off in the long run. People will look at you differently because you have changed your ways have changed. Not because you have changed as a person, but because your ways of approaching life with a different swag as I call it. Different style. You may even get made fun of in a negative way saying you may have forgotten about them. Remember always that when at the bottom some may want you to stay at the bottom because it makes them feel like they are doing something right or because it may make them feel better.

Your success may make them look bad. You may have to learn to avoid old crowds and surround yourself with people who are succeeding in life. Who want more than just sitting around and doing nothing to get ahead or out of their current situation. Always remember there are some people who came from that same bottom you came from and sometimes don't understand what the bottom is because they were not raised in certain ways you have. Everybody's path is different depending on where you want to get to and can relate to one another in some shape, form, fashion, or size and all have the ultimate goal and that is too successful. Don't forget on the way to the top what was said to get from the bottom of whom who have said it. When you didn't have it. When you was struggling to find a way out. Some may even come up with lies so people can believe them. Stay focused and use those negative saying as energy that will fuel your ambition. Inspiration to live and motivation to do more. Just a dream you may one day wake up from. Your labor that you paved the way.

Music sounds different now and the air tastes refreshing. You will gain followers positively. Always appreciate what one does for you along your path and the cause they do things for. Love you or not but never be used People may even try to succeed off your success. Some may even want to ride in the same car as you are in. Some may even praise your name only to gain something personal from it. Instead of asking they manipulate. Instead of helping they may try to make fun of you.

Chapter 31
A Change is Good.

Your ambition and your power. You may even want to change your name for a new beginning. A fresh start. That drive becomes more powerful. You move in a more militant way. You are more focused than before or when you started. Your stride is longer. Dreams start to appear with every move. Things that were once hard is a little easier.

Sitting back you must look at all the hard work you have done and where it's brought you to. You may have been in the hole. You may have been in the closet. Life is a double-edged sword. Holding it is not easy, but all you have to do is close your mouth and listen more.

Listen to all the signs and warnings. Illegal punches. Low blows. Watch all things and people knowing their intentions may not all be positive or in your favor. Watch all ditches and pot holes knowing they all cannot be avoided. Attempt not to repeat the same ways or moves that are negative. Take a different way back home or where you came from. Smokescreen those who are aware of your path, and they want to join you because of your success. Dilute the water in which your haters drink. Ignore the words that may be heart-breaking. Words that do not motivate you or help you in your path to success. Know in the end of the path you have chosen, you will see what you have built all through elevation and destroying all which you have stood for.

Truth By Roderick Howard

The foundation that has been laid down and the house that has been built high enough to reach the clouds. Not to be blown away, but just out of the reach of those who want to see you fail. Those who want to see you accomplish nothing that would allow you to move forward. Those who want to see you forget what you pray for or forget how much support you may have. You have those who may plot against your wishes. Just keep your mind focused on your goals. Keep your hands clean from illegal substances, movements and clear from the blurred vision that may not allow you to see what is in front of you. Even when success is near; still push for more. Even if money is made and you may feel a little comfortable; strive for more.

Feel free from trouble. Feel free from worries. Rain does not always bring on a gloomy day. The air that blows with the winds of nature feel so refreshing that the breath inhaled and exhaled are deep. You may feel at that moment anything can be accomplished, and that is true. Even when situations are tight and things become stressful. Let it rain on your face and look to the sky and let your thoughts of stress and expression be released into what we inhale as air and exhale what feeds the trees. The circle of life we say all bonds with each other. Nature takes its course and rules the land which we love. The earth will rotate, the stars will always glow electrons, and will always move, and ether will always burn.

Love life to the fullest and appreciate all things positive that come your way. God loves all and all are his children even if we know it or not.

www.ingramcontent.com/pod-product-compliance
Lightning Source LLC
Chambersburg PA
CBHW052136270326
41930CB00012B/2909